Amazon S3 Essentials

Get started with Amazon S3 for virtually unlimited cloud
and Internet storage

Sunil Gulabani

BIRMINGHAM - MUMBAI

Amazon S3 Essentials

First published: October 2015

Production reference: 1261015

Published by Packt Publishing Ltd.
Livery Place
35 Livery Street
Birmingham B3 2PB, UK.

ISBN 978-1-78355-489-8

www.packtpub.com

Credits

Author
Sunil Gulabani

Reviewers
Guðmundur Jón Halldórsson
Parth Mehta

Commissioning Editor
Kunal Parikh

Acquisition Editors
Shaon Basu
Sonali Vernekar

Content Development Editor
Mayur Pawanikar

Technical Editor
Humera Shaikh

Copy Editors
Shruti Iyer
Sonia Mathur

Project Coordinator
Kranti Berde

Proofreader
Safis Editing

Indexer
Monica Ajmera Mehta

Production Coordinator
Nilesh R. Mohite

Cover Work
Nilesh R. Mohite

About the Author

Sunil Gulabani is a software engineer based in Ahmedabad, Gujarat, and author of the book, *Developing RESTful Web Services with Jersey 2.0, Packt Publishing*. He completed his graduation in commerce from S M Patel Institute of Commerce (SMPIC) and obtained his master's degree in computer applications from AES Institute of Computer Studies (AESICS). Sunil presented a paper entitled *Effective Label Matching For Automated Evaluation of Use Case Diagrams* at an IEEE conference on Technology For Education (T4E) held at IIIT Hyderabad, along with senior lecturers, Vinay Vachharajani and Dr. Jyoti Pareek.

Since 2011, he has been working as a software engineer and is a cloud technology–savvy person. Sunil is experienced in developing enterprise solutions using Java Enterprise Edition. He has a keen interest in system architecture and integration, data modeling, relational databases, and mapping with NoSQL for high throughput.

Apart from this, Sunil is interested in writing tech blogs and is actively involved in knowledge-sharing communities.

You can visit him online at `http://www.sunilgulabani.com` and follow him on Twitter at `twitter.com/sunil_gulabani`. You can also reach Sunil directly at `sunil_gulabani@yahoo.com`.

I would like to express my heartiest thanks to my parents, my wife, Priya, and family members, who supported me at each and every level of my career. I would also like to convey thanks to my friends and colleagues, without whom jumping onto the next step of my career would not be possible. Also, thanks to the Packt Publishing team, who gave me the opportunity to author this book.

About the Reviewers

Guðmundur Jón Halldórsson is a veteran software developer who has designed and built software for many of the biggest companies in Iceland. His focus is on finding big data solutions for his company.

Guðmundur is the chief technology officer of Medilync, a small medical device company in Iceland. Medilync was founded with the goal of revolutionizing the way diabetes is managed and treated in a value-based care landscape.

Guðmundur is the author of *Apache Accumulo for Developers, Packt Publishing*.

> I want to thank my family because without them I would be lost.

Parth Mehta is a full stack software developer and earned his bachelor's degree in information technology from Vishwakarma Government Engineering College (VGEC).

He is an Oracle Certified Java programmer and also has experience in development and deployment of scalable and highly available application design with Advanced Java technologies and frameworks, Amazon Web Services, SOA with REST, and AngularJS.

Parth is passionate about learning algorithm design and development and a big fan of the book, *The Algorithm Design Manual*. He can be reached at parthmehta009@gmail.com.

www.PacktPub.com

Support files, eBooks, discount offers, and more

For support files and downloads related to your book, please visit www.PacktPub.com.

Did you know that Packt offers eBook versions of every book published, with PDF and ePub files available? You can upgrade to the eBook version at www.PacktPub.com and as a print book customer, you are entitled to a discount on the eBook copy. Get in touch with us at service@packtpub.com for more details.

At www.PacktPub.com, you can also read a collection of free technical articles, sign up for a range of free newsletters and receive exclusive discounts and offers on Packt books and eBooks.

https://www2.packtpub.com/books/subscription/packtlib

Do you need instant solutions to your IT questions? PacktLib is Packt's online digital book library. Here, you can search, access, and read Packt's entire library of books.

Why subscribe?
- Fully searchable across every book published by Packt
- Copy and paste, print, and bookmark content
- On demand and accessible via a web browser

Free access for Packt account holders

If you have an account with Packt at www.PacktPub.com, you can use this to access PacktLib today and view 9 entirely free books. Simply use your login credentials for immediate access.

Table of Contents

Preface

The Amazon Simple Storage Service (Amazon S3) is an online object storage service. It can be used to store and get any data via the following:

- The REST web service interface
- The SOAP web service interface
- BitTorrent

Amazon S3 is easy to configure; it's a reliable and scalable storage that stores files (objects) with high security at a nominal price. Developers or system teams don't have to worry about the data that is stored at or retrieved from Amazon S3. Amazon S3 manages the web-scale computing by itself.

What this book covers

Chapter 1, *Know-How about S3*, gives a brief introduction to Amazon S3, covering the basic concepts, buckets, objects, and keys. We will also discuss the features of Amazon S3 that can be utilized at minimal cost and its reliable storage service.

Chapter 2, *S3 using the AWS Management Console*, teaches you how to use AWS Management Console and manage buckets, folders, objects, and operations on it. Along with basic operations, you will also learn about logging and versioning.

Chapter 3, *S3 using AWS SDK – Java (Part 1)*, shows you how to use Amazon SDK—Java for Amazon S3 web services. We will take a look at how to create, upload, get, and delete the bucket, folder, and objects.

Chapter 4, *S3 using AWS SDK – Java (Part 2)*, explains how to copy objects. It discusses multipart copy objects, which are used for large object sizes; the bucket life cycle, which defines two ways—transition (moving to Glacier) and removal; and CORS configuration, which is used to provide access via different domains.

Chapter 5, Deploying a Website on S3, shows how to configure static website hosting along with the bucket. We will consider how to map our custom domain name with the bucket.

What you need for this book

You need the following for this book:

- An understanding of Java
- The Eclipse IDE
- A browser (compatible with Amazon Management Console)

Who this book is for

This book is intended for system engineers or developers, software architects, project managers, and users who want to explore Amazon S3 SDK Java. If you want to learn about Amazon S3 quickly, then this book is for you. Basic knowledge of Java programming is expected.

Conventions

In this book, you will find a number of text styles that distinguish between different kinds of information. Here are some examples of these styles and an explanation of their meaning.

Code words in text, database table names, folder names, filenames, file extensions, pathnames, dummy URLs, user input, and Twitter handles are shown as follows: "Replace bucketName with the actual bucket name and OBJECT_KEY_OR_FOLDER_NAME with either your object key or the name of the folder which is supposed to be deleted."

A block of code is set as follows:

```
package com.chapter3;

import java.util.Date;

import com.amazonaws.AmazonClientException;
import com.amazonaws.AmazonServiceException;
import com.amazonaws.services.s3.model.Bucket;

public class CreateBucket   extends AmazonS3ClientInitializer{
  public CreateBucket() {
```

```
    super();
  }

  public static void main(String[] args) {
    String bucketName = "sg-bucket-2015-using-java-api-" + new
      Date().getTime();

    CreateBucket object = new CreateBucket();
    object.createBucket(bucketName);
    object.listBucket();
  }

  public void createBucket(String bucketName){
    System.out.println("================ Create Bucket
      ================ ");
    try {
      System.out.println("Bucket Name: " + bucketName + "\n");
      s3.createBucket(bucketName);
    } catch (AmazonServiceException exception) {
      exception.printStackTrace();
    } catch (AmazonClientException exception) {
      exception.printStackTrace();
    }
  }

  public void listBucket(){
    System.out.println("================ Listing Buckets
      ================ ");
    for (Bucket bucket : s3.listBuckets()) {
      System.out.println(" - " + bucket.getName());
    }
  }
}
```

When we wish to draw your attention to a particular part of a code block, the relevant lines or items are set in bold:

```
BucketVersioningConfiguration configuration = new
  BucketVersioningConfiguration(BucketVersioningConfiguration.
    ENABLED);

SetBucketVersioningConfigurationRequest request = new
  SetBucketVersioningConfigurationRequest(bucketName, configuration);

s3.setBucketVersioningConfiguration(request);
```

New terms and **important words** are shown in bold. Words that you see on the screen, for example, in menus or dialog boxes, appear in the text like this: "Click on the **Create New Group** button."

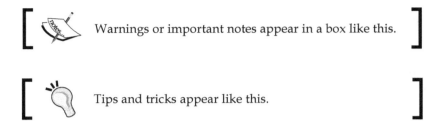

> Warnings or important notes appear in a box like this.

> Tips and tricks appear like this.

Reader feedback

Feedback from our readers is always welcome. Let us know what you think about this book—what you liked or disliked. Reader feedback is important for us as it helps us develop titles that you will really get the most out of.

To send us general feedback, simply e-mail feedback@packtpub.com, and mention the book's title in the subject of your message.

If there is a topic that you have expertise in and you are interested in either writing or contributing to a book, see our author guide at www.packtpub.com/authors.

Customer support

Now that you are the proud owner of a Packt book, we have a number of things to help you to get the most from your purchase.

Downloading the example code

You can download the example code files from your account at http://www.packtpub.com for all the Packt Publishing books you have purchased. If you purchased this book elsewhere, you can visit http://www.packtpub.com/support and register to have the files e-mailed directly to you.

Downloading the color images of this book

We also provide you with a PDF file that has color images of the screenshots/diagrams used in this book. The color images will help you better understand the changes in the output. You can download this file from: https://www.packtpub.com/sites/default/files/downloads/4898OS_Graphics.pdf.

Errata

Although we have taken every care to ensure the accuracy of our content, mistakes do happen. If you find a mistake in one of our books—maybe a mistake in the text or the code—we would be grateful if you could report this to us. By doing so, you can save other readers from frustration and help us improve subsequent versions of this book. If you find any errata, please report them by visiting http://www.packtpub.com/submit-errata, selecting your book, clicking on the **Errata Submission Form** link, and entering the details of your errata. Once your errata are verified, your submission will be accepted and the errata will be uploaded to our website or added to any list of existing errata under the Errata section of that title.

To view the previously submitted errata, go to https://www.packtpub.com/books/content/support and enter the name of the book in the search field. The required information will appear under the **Errata** section.

Piracy

Piracy of copyrighted material on the Internet is an ongoing problem across all media. At Packt, we take the protection of our copyright and licenses very seriously. If you come across any illegal copies of our works in any form on the Internet, please provide us with the location address or website name immediately so that we can pursue a remedy.

Please contact us at copyright@packtpub.com with a link to the suspected pirated material.

We appreciate your help in protecting our authors and our ability to bring you valuable content.

Questions

If you have a problem with any aspect of this book, you can contact us at questions@packtpub.com, and we will do our best to address the problem.

1
Know-How about S3

The **Amazon Simple Storage Service (Amazon S3)** is an online object storage. It can be used to store and get any data via the following:

- REST web service interface
- SOAP web service interface
- BitTorrent

Amazon S3 is easy to configure, and is a reliable and scalable storage that stores files (objects) at a nominal pricing along with high security. Neither the developers nor the system team have to worry about the data that is stored at or retrieved from Amazon S3. Amazon S3 manages the Web-Scale computing by itself.

The following concepts will be covered in this chapter:

- The need for S3 and its advantages
- Basic concepts of Amazon S3
- Features of Amazon S3
- Security
- Integration
- Use cases

The need for S3 and its advantages

Amazon S3 can be used for storing data for application usage as well as for backing up and archiving the data. It doesn't bind the files to be stored. We can store any file, which are treated as objects, in Amazon S3. Amazon uses S3 to run its own global network of websites (`http://docs.aws.amazon.com/AmazonS3/latest/dev/Welcome.html`).

We can store as much data as we want in Amazon S3; it doesn't restrict a user from storing any. Amazon charges the user for the storage that is actually used. So, it is quite inexpensive for the user, because he/she doesn't need to purchase storage externally.

Amazon S3 keeps the redundant data across multiple data centers for high scalability. The user can select the region where his/her data will be stored. This reduces the latency in storing and retrieving the data. Amazon S3 also offers security on the objects. The user can make the object publicly or privately accessible. We can also store encrypted data in Amazon S3, and it guarantees a server uptime of 99.9 percent.

Amazon S3 can be integrated with any application or services offered by Amazon, such as **Amazon Elastic Compute Cloud (Amazon EC2)**, **Amazon Elastic Block Storage (Amazon EBS)**, Amazon Glacier, and so on.

Subscribing to Amazon S3 is free, and you just need to pay for the bandwidth that you use and for whatever you are actually hosting. Small start-ups usually don't have an infrastructure to store their huge amount data. So, they opt for Amazon S3 to store their images, videos, files, and so on to minimize the costs.

Amazon S3 also provides website hosting services. You can directly upload your pages in Amazon S3, and map it to your domain.

Basic concepts of Amazon S3

Let's take a look at the basic S3 concepts:

Buckets

A bucket is a container in Amazon S3 where the files are uploaded. For using Amazon S3 to store a file, you need to create at least one bucket. Files (objects) are stored in buckets.

The following are a few features of buckets:

- The bucket name should be unique because it is shared by all users.
- Buckets can contain logical nested folders and subfolders. But it cannot contain nested buckets.
- You can create a maximum of 100 buckets in a single account.
- The bucket name can contain letters, numbers, periods, dash, and the underscore.
- The bucket name should start with a letter or number, and it should be between 3 to 25 characters long.

Buckets can be managed via the following:

- REST-style HTTP interface
- SOAP interface

The following bucket looks similar to the Amazon S3 bucket to which we will upload files (objects):

A bucket doesn't have any size restrictions for the user. It can store objects of any size.

Buckets can be accessed via HTTP URLs as follows:

- `http://< BUCKET_NAME>.s3.amazonaws.com/< OBJECT_NAME >`
- `http://s3.amazonaws.com/< BUCKET_NAME >/< OBJECT_NAME >`

In the preceding URLs, `BUCKET_NAME` will be the name of the bucket that you provided while creating it. And `OBJECT_NAME` will be the name of the object that you provided while creating the object.

Objects

An object is a stored file in Amazon S3. Each object consists of a unique identifier, the user who uploaded the object, and permissions for other users to perform CRUD operations on it. Every object is stored in a bucket.

Objects can be managed via the following:

- REST-style HTTP interface
- SOAP interface

Objects can be downloaded via the following:

- HTTP GET interface
- BitTorrent protocol

The bucket can consist of any type of object, be it a PDF, text, video, audio, or any other kind of files.

Keys

While creating an object, a key will be assigned to the object. This key will be used for retrieving the object. The key should have the following features:

- Be unique in the bucket
- Contain alphabets, numbers, and special characters such as -, !, _, ., *, ', (, and)

Features of Amazon S3

The following are the main features of Amazon S3:

- **Allows website hosting**: Amazon S3 allows users to host a website and map it to their domain. This is very cost effective, because the user pays only for what he/she uses. Moreover, the user doesn't require highly configured servers to serve the website.

- **Scalable**: Amazon S3 doesn't restrict the user to any size limit for storing data. As it is a pay-as-you-go service, it stores the data, and the bill is generated accordingly. So the subscriber never faces a lack of space.

- **Reliable**: Amazon S3 guarantees a server uptime of 99.9 percent. Therefore, the subscriber does not need to worry about data reliability.

- **Security**: Amazon S3 provides a strong authentication mechanism where the stored data can be manipulated.

- **Standard interfaces**: Amazon S3 provides the **Representational State Transfer (REST)** and **Simple Object Access Protocol (SOAP)** web services that can be consumed by any web framework.

- **Reduced Redundancy Storage**: Amazon S3 provides the subscribers with an optional feature for storing data with the **Reduced Redundancy Storage (RRS)** storage class. It is basically used for storing non-critical and reproducible data at lower levels of redundancy. The cost of storing on an RRS storage class is quite less as compared to the standard storage class.

- **Torrent tracking and seeding**: Amazon S3 can act as a torrent tracker, and seed the files from your machine.

- **Share the data with a temporary URL**: Amazon S3 provides the subscriber the ability to share a URL, which auto-expires after a period of time. This helps the subscriber in sharing the data for a minimal period of time. Other users cannot use that data after the URL expires.

- **Logging**: It provides the logging of all activities that are performed on bucket. This makes it easy for the subscriber to audit the activities on the bucket if he so wishes. Generally, when a subscriber hosts a website on Amazon S3, he enables the logging feature to track the activities.

- **Versioning**: Amazon S3 allows storing of multiple versions of an object. It is basically used for recovering old data that is lost unintentionally.

- **Security**: Amazon S3 provides security on buckets and objects. While creating the buckets, you can provide access control lists for other users of the bucket who can create, update, delete, or list objects. You can even set the geographical location of your data.

- **Integration**: Amazon S3 can be integrated with several other services such as Amazon EC2, Amazon EBS, Amazon Glacier, and many other applications. Generally, developers use Amazon S3 for storing images, videos, or documents, and for accessing them via HTTP Get.

Case studies

The Amazon S3 can be utilized for different purposes:

- **File hosting**: Companies often deploy their images, videos, audios, PDFs, DOCs, and other files in Amazon S3. This helps in loading the files directly from Amazon S3 without managing the on-premise infrastructure.

- **Storing data on mobile-based applications**: Many users/companies go for Amazon S3 to store mobile app data. This becomes easy for user/companies to manage mobile user data over Amazon S3.

- **Static website hosting**: Users can host their static website over Amazon S3 along with Amazon Route53.

- **Video Hosting**: Companies upload their videos over Amazon S3, which can then be accessed on their website. Amazon S3 can also be configured to provide video streaming.

- **Backup**: Users can keep a backup of their data, which will be securely and reliably stored in Amazon S3. Amazon S3 can also be configured to move the old data over to Amazon Glacier for archiving, as the Glacier costs less as compared to S3.

Use cases

Let's now see how Amazon S3 can be used in a project.

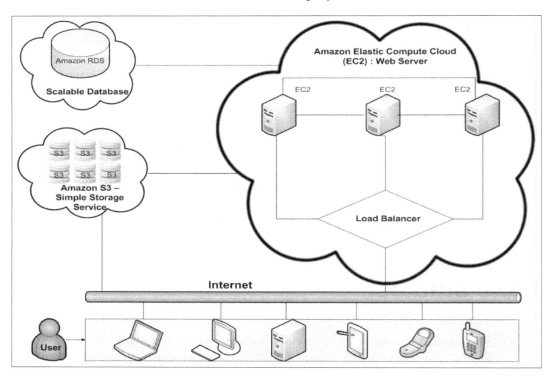

In the preceding diagram we have the following:

- The **Amazon Elastic Compute Cloud (EC2)** machines where the application is deployed.

- The Amazon **Load Balancer** will be responsible for redirecting the user request to specific applications deployed on the EC2 machines.

- The **Amazon Relational Database Service (RDS)** is used for storing application data. It provides scalability, durability, and an easy-to-manage database service.

- Amazon S3 where the image/audio/video files are stored.

- And lastly, the front devices like a laptop, desktop, or mobile applications that send requests to the application.

The preceding example is a sample case study. There are various ways for integrating Amazon S3 in our application.

Summary

In this chapter, we introduced Amazon S3, and covered the basic concepts—buckets, objects, and keys. We explored the basic features of Amazon S3, which help in providing a reliable storage service at minimal cost. Amazon S3 can be consumed by startups, individual developers, or big size companies for data storage, backups for recovery, and so on. Amazon S3 also provides an extensibility for integration with other Amazon services and many other applications. In the next chapter, you will learn how to utilize the AWS S3 basic services like buckets, folders, and objects.

2
S3 using the AWS Management Console

The AWS Management Console is a browser-based graphical user interface in which users can manage the resources at Amazon Web Services.

The AWS Management Console supports the following browsers:

- Firefox
- Chrome
- Internet Explorer
- Safari

The AWS Management Console mobile app is also available on iOS and Android.

In this chapter, we will focus on manipulating the AWS console. We will interact with Amazon S3 using the AWS Management Console. AWS provides a **Graphical User Interface** (**GUI**) to manage Amazon S3 resources and tasks, so it is easier to understand and configure as per our needs. We will take a detailed look into managing buckets, objects, and the operations that can be performed on the objects.

We will cover the following topics in this chapter:

- Logging in to the AWS Management Console
- Bucket operations
- Folder operations
- Object operations
- Versioning

Logging in to the AWS Management Console

To log in to the AWS Management Console, go to `http://aws.amazon.com/` and click on **AWS Management Console**, as shown in the following screenshot:

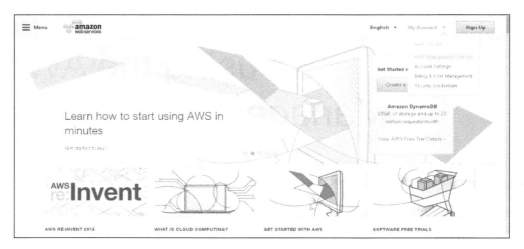

Sign in using your credentials:

[If you are a new user, you can opt for the free trial account.]

All the AWS services are listed on the landing page. Click on **S3** (highlighted in the following screenshot):

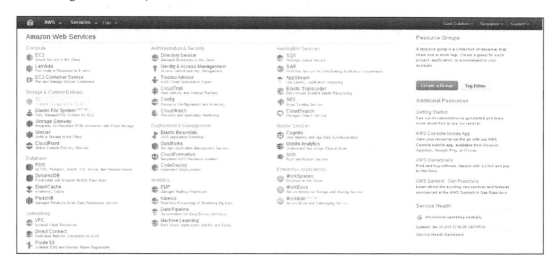

Clicking on **S3** will direct you to the Amazon S3 Console. We can manage the bucket here:

Bucket operations

A bucket is a container in Amazon S3 into which files are uploaded. To use Amazon S3 to store a file, you need to create at least one bucket. The bucket name should be unique because it is shared by all users. Files (objects) are stored in buckets. Buckets can contain nested folders and subfolders. But they cannot contain nested buckets. You can create a maximum of 100 buckets in a single account.

The bucket name that you specify can contain letters, numbers, periods, and dashes. The name should start with a letter or a number, and it should be between 3 characters and 63 characters long. A bucket doesn't restrict the user to a size limit.

Click on the **Create Bucket** button seen in the preceding screenshot, and a dialog box for creating a bucket pops up, as shown in the following image:

We created a bucket named `sg-bucket-2015`, with the region as **Singapore**; Amazon S3 allows us to create region-specific buckets. This will also be the region from where your Amazon S3 objects will primarily be accessed. Currently, you can select any of the regions given in the following list:

- **US Standard**
- **Oregon**
- **Northern California**
- **Ireland**
- **Singapore**
- **Tokyo**
- **Sydney**

- **Sao Paulo**
- **Frankfurt**

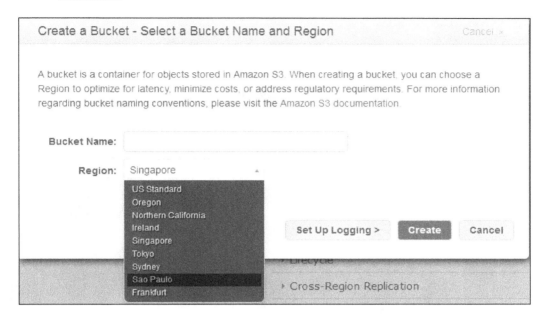

You can see the name of the bucket that we created and its properties displayed on the screen. Once you create a bucket, you cannot rename it.

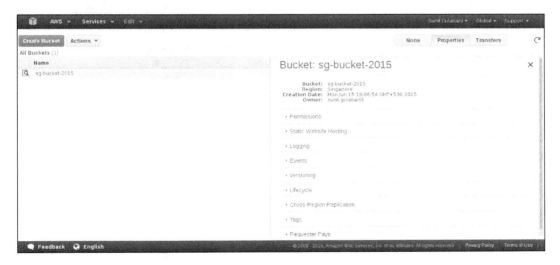

While creating the bucket, you can also enable access logging. This logging mechanism can be used to track bucket requests. It provides details regarding each access request, such as the request type, the resources being utilized, and the date and time when the request was made. This logging mechanism is optional and is disabled by default.

Amazon S3 does not charge anything for using the logging mechanism. It just charges for the storage used by the log that is generated.

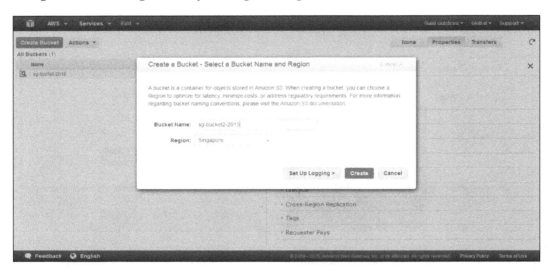

Click on **Set up Logging** in the **Properties** section of the bucket to navigate to the following screen:

In the **Create a Bucket - Select a Bucket Name and Region** dialog box, select the **Enabled** checkbox, select the bucket for which logging needs to be enabled, and enter the prefix for the server access log to be generated:

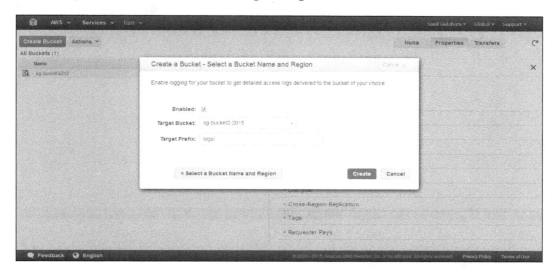

You can even check and change the logging mechanism, as seen in the following screenshot:

If you check inside the bucket, you can see that a log folder has been created:

Log files are generated inside the log folder. Whatever operations are performed on the bucket can be seen in this folder:

Moving back to the bucket, we are provided with two options:

- **Create Folder…**
- **Upload**

Folder operations

The folders in Amazon S3 are S3 files that are used to put Amazon S3 objects together under one group. The S3 folders are similar to the file system in computers. Nested folders can be created. Permissions can also be levied on folders, as in the case of Amazon S3 objects. Folders are just treated as a prefix to the objects — they are used as the key name prefix for the objects.

As you can see in the preceding screenshot, we have created a folder named **sg-folder**. Once the folder name is given, you cannot rename it. You can create and delete folders. You can even make a folder and its objects accessible to the public.

As seen in the preceding screenshot, under the folder tab, we have an option to:

- **Create Folder...**
- **Upload**

So, using the **Create Folder...** option, we can create folders within the folder.

A folder can be made publicly accessible by clicking on the **Make Public** option:

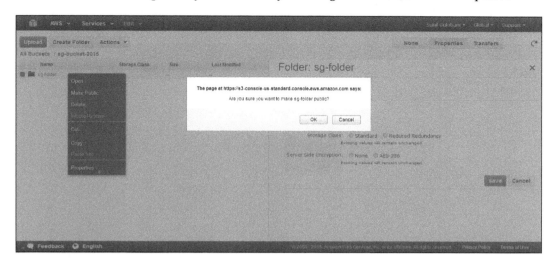

You can delete the folder when you don't need it anymore, as shown in the following screenshot:

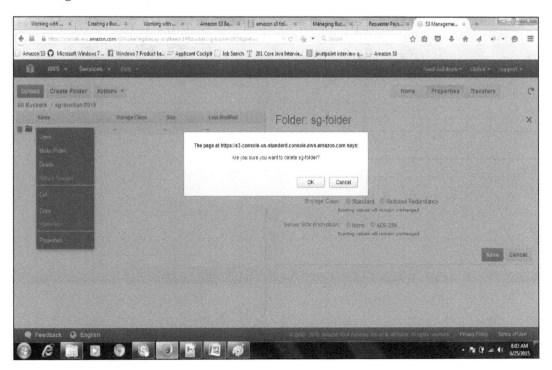

Object operations

In the bucket/folder section, there is an option to create a folder or upload an object:

Clicking on **Upload** displays a pop-up window, which allows the user to select the **Add Files** or **Upload Folder** options using **Enable Enhanced Uploader (BETA)**:

We added the files `index.html`, `index-1.html`, and `index-2.html` using **Add Files**. Look at the listing of the files under the `sg-folder` folder in the following screenshot:

While adding files, you can also set the details, permissions, and metadata for the group of files that is being added. However, you can even set the details, permissions, and metadata after the files have been uploaded.

There are two options under the **Set Details** section:

- **Use Reduced Redundancy Storage**
- **Use Server Side Encryption**

Use Reduced Redundancy Storage

Amazon S3 provides the subscribers an optional feature for storing data with the RRS storage class. It is basically for storing non-critical and reproducible data at lower levels of redundancy. The cost of storing using an RRS storage class is less as compared to using the standard storage class.

Use Server Side Encryption

This is used to provide security. Amazon S3 encrypts an object when you add data. This encryption process is processed at the data centers. When a user accesses the object, Amazon S3 decrypts the data and sends it to the user. The **Use Server Side Encryption** feature has two options:

- **Use the Amazon S3 service master key**
- **Use an AWS Key Management Service master key**

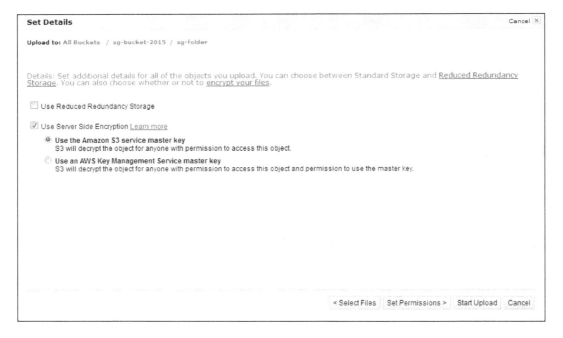

In the **Set Permissions** section, the **Grant me full control** permission option is enabled by default. By selecting the **Make everything public** checkbox, any user can access the objects without any authorization:

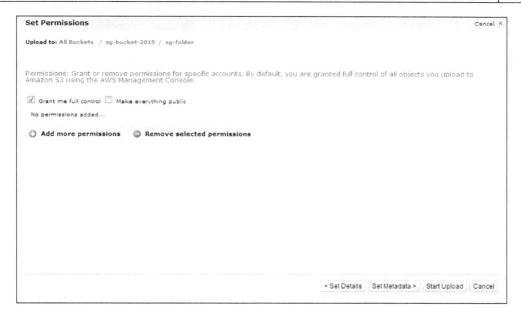

On clicking on **Add more permissions**, a new permission row will be added where you can assign the **Open/Download, View Permissions**, and **Edit Permissions** options to **Grantee**.

For **Grantee**, you can add the e-mail address of the AWS user or a canonical ID of the Amazon S3 group. A maximum number of 100 grantees can be defined.

In the **Set Metadata** section, Amazon assigns the content type of the object automatically by default. Apart from that, you can define the key-value pair for the object. You can assign some of the predefined metadata, and if you need to assign user-defined metadata, you can create it with the **x-amz-meta-** key as the prefix:

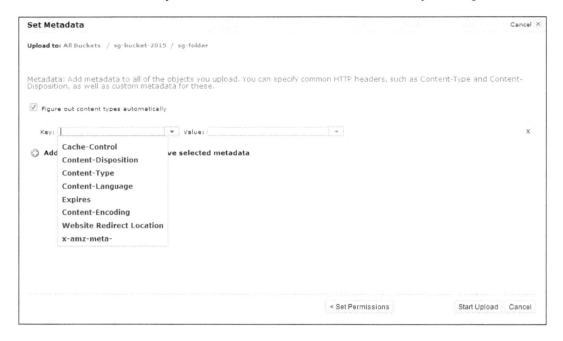

Now let's try to access the `index.html` file. Our file is at `https://s3-ap-southeast-1.amazonaws.com/sg-bucket-2015/sg-folder/index.html` or at `http://sg-bucket-2015.s3.amazonaws.com/sg-folder/index.html`.

In the preceding URL, `sg-bucket-2015` is the bucket name, `sg-folder` is the name of the folder created under the `sg-bucket-2015` bucket, and `index.html` is the object.

When we try to access the URL, we get the access denied message:

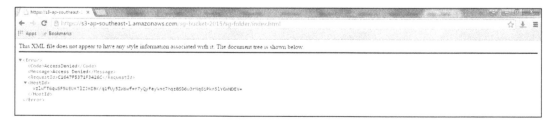

We are unable to access the object because we haven't provided access to a specific user or the public. Let's make the `index.html` object publicly accessible so that we can view it:

Now that we have made the `index.html` object publicly accessible, we'll open the `https://s3-ap-southeast-1.amazonaws.com/sg-bucket-2015/sg-folder/index.html` or `http://sg-bucket-2015.s3.amazonaws.com/sg-folder/index.html` URL in the browser:

To delete the object, right-click on the object, and click on **Delete**:

Versioning

Versioning enables us to store different versions of an object. It helps us to store, retrieve, and restore old objects. This can be useful when we accidentally delete or modify an object. In such a case, we can restore the last stable object. If we delete an object, Amazon S3 inserts a delete marker for that object rather than deleting it permanently. If we overwrite the object, Amazon S3 creates a new version of the same.

Versioning can be done in any of the following states:

- Unversioned — the default
- Versioning enabled
- Versioning-suspended

To enable versioning, click on the bucket and under the **Properties** tab, click on the **Versioning** tree:

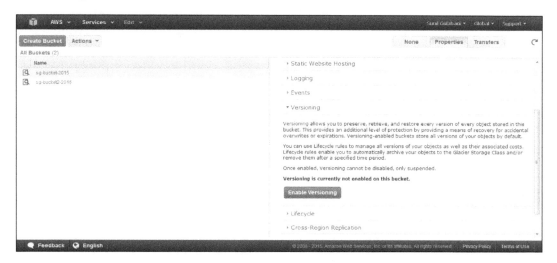

When we click on **Enable Versioning**, it asks for confirmation. Since storing many versions of an object would cost a lot, it is better to define the lifecycle rules for the object.

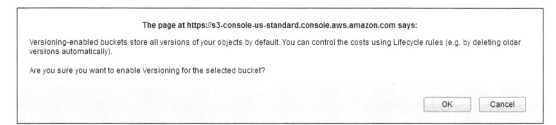

Summary

In this chapter, we learned to manage a bucket, a folder, an object and the operations performed upon an object. Logging and versioning needs to be carefully taken into consideration. Amazon S3 charges the user for storing data. If your data generates more logs, or if your object has a number of versions, your cost of using Amazon S3 goes up. So be careful while configuring it.

In the next chapter, you will learn to use S3 with the Java SDK.

3
S3 using AWS SDK – Java (Part 1)

The Amazon S3 SDK for Java provides an extensive API handling system for consuming Amazon S3. The API can be used to store and fetch data over the Internet. A frontend user sees what your application displays, and you can add, fetch, or delete images, audio, video, or any file to and from Amazon S3 using the API at the backend.

The Amazon S3 SDK gives control to the developers for creating high-end applications. Developers need not worry about the files that are stored on Amazon S3 as they are all managed by Amazon.

Let's see how to manage Amazon S3 using the Amazon SDK–Java.

Prerequisites

The following sections will explain the prerequisites for managing Amazon S3 using the AWS SDK for Java.

The AWS SDK for Java

The AWS SDK for Java is required in order to use the Amazon API. This SDK contains a .jar file, which we need to add to our project's classpath. You can download the SDK from the following URL:

```
http://aws.amazon.com/sdk-for-java
```

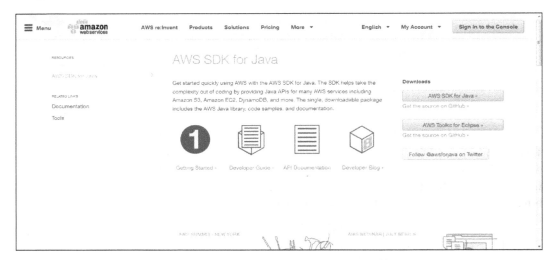

The access key and secret key

The access key and the secret key are required to connect to Amazon S3. These credentials can be obtained by creating a user in Amazon IAM.

Log in to the AWS console, and click on **Identity & Access Management**, as shown in the following screenshot:

This directs you to the **Identity & Access Management** screen, which enables you to create AWS users and groups, and assign roles to them, as seen in the following screenshot:

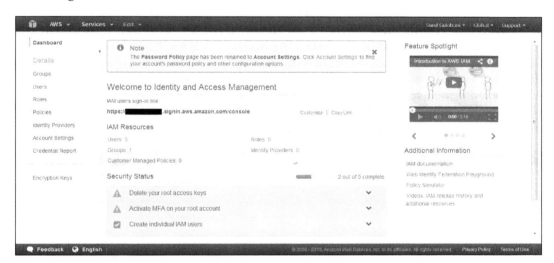

Click on **Users** in the menu on the left-hand side of the screen. This opens up a screen for creating new users and for displaying the listing of the existing users:

Click on the **Create New Users** tab, which directs you to the **Create User** dialog box.

The **Create User** dialog box allows the creation of five users at a time, thus making it easier for the administrator to create many users in one go. An option for access key generation is also given on the screen. This option is selected for users who are granted the permission to use SDK, which requires the access and secret keys. It is not selected if the users are only allowed to access the AWS console. The username should have a maximum length of 64 characters. After entering the username, click on the **Create** button:

As you can see in the preceding screenshot, three users and their security credentials have been created. You need to save these security credentials in a secure place so that no one else can use them. The security credentials will remain available at this place only. If you misplace the security credentials, you will need to create another user, and use the newly generated security credentials.

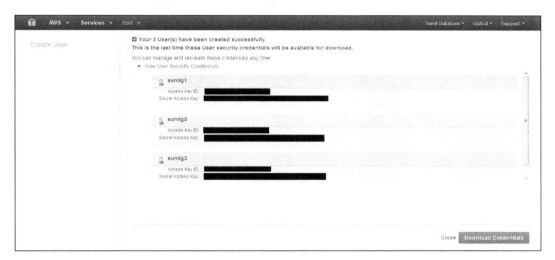

The following screenshot displays the list of users including the newly created ones:

Creating a group and attaching the AmazonS3FullAccess policy

We will now create a group and assign **AmazonS3FullAccess** to it so that we can manage Amazon S3 using the Amazon S3 API.

Click on **Groups** in the menu on the left-hand side of the **Identity & Access Management** screen:

Click on the **Create New Group** button. This prompts you to enter the group name in step 1. As you can see in the following screenshot, we have entered `Developers` as the **Group Name** so that it can be identified easily. The group name can have a maximum of 128 characters.

Step 2 is **Attach Policy**. Here we will select the policy that this group will have. This implies that any user who has been added to this group can access only those services that are attached as policy to that group. This limits the user access as per his/her control access policy. Select **AmazonS3FullAccess**, as shown in the following screenshot, so that you can add, update, get, and delete objects:

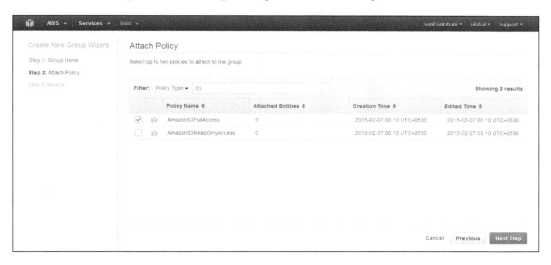

Step 3 is for reviewing the group name and the attached policies. After reviewing, click on the **Create Group** button:

Once the group has been created, select the **Developers** group, and select the **Add Users to Group** option under the **Group Actions** menu:

This takes you to the **Add Users to Group** section. Select the users that you want to add to this group, and click on the **Add Users** button:

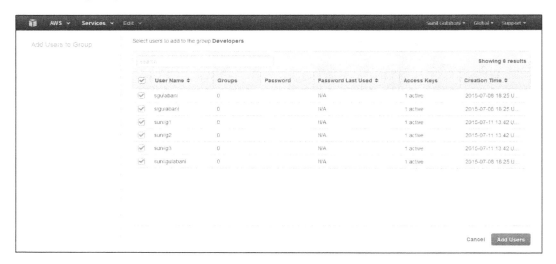

Now we are done with the prerequisites. We will now move on to coding where the actual operations are going to be performed. Yay!

Initialization

We need the AWS credentials to access Amazon Web Services for using the API tools. We will check out two ways to get an instance of `com.amazonaws.auth.AWSCredentials`:

- Using `BasicAWSCredentials`
- Using `ProfileCredentialsProvider`

Using BasicAWSCredentials

`BasicAWSCredentials` is a vanilla flavor implementation class for providing the AWS credentials, which are the access key and the secret key:

```
// Class Variable
protected AWSCredentials credentials = null;

. . . .

public void initializeAWSCredentials(){
  credentials = new BasicAWSCredentials("ACCESS_ID",
    "SECRET_KEY");
}
```

Replace `ACCESS_ID` and `SECRET_KEY` with your actual access id and secret key.

Using ProfileCredentialsProvider

`ProfileCredentialsProvider` provides `AWSCredentials`. It accesses the configuration file and looks for the named profile credentials. This helps in storing multiple credentials in the configuration file, and in using the profile based on the name provided by the application.

The configuration file on my machine (Linux) is located at `/home/sunil/.aws/credentials`.

For a Windows machine, it is located at `C:\Users\SUNIL\.aws\credentials`.

```
// Class Variable
protected AWSCredentials credentials = null;

. . . .

public void initializeAWSCredentials(){
  credentials = new ProfileCredentialsProvider("NAMED_PROFILE").
getCredentials();
}
```

Replace `NAMED_PROFILE` with your actual profile name that exists in the configuration file.

If the access key is invalid, an exception is thrown with the following message:

```
The AWS Access Key Id you provided does not exist in our records.
```

The following error code is also displayed:

```
InvalidAccessKeyId
```

The best part about Amazon API is the exception handling mechanism, by which a developer can easily trace the error exactly.

Next we need to create the instance of `AmazonS3Client` that will actually interact with Amazon S3 Web Services. The `AmazonS3Client` instance is the main class, which we use for storing, modifying, getting, or deleting buckets/folders/objects and their properties:

```java
// Class Variable
protected AmazonS3 s3;

....

s3 = new AmazonS3Client(credentials);

Region region = Region.getRegion(Regions.AP_SOUTHEAST_1);
s3.setRegion(region);
```

In the preceding code snippet, we created an instance of `AmazonS3Client` in which we provided the previously created `AWSCredentials` instance. Apart from this, we've set a region for `AmazonS3Client` as well so that whichever services we use for Amazon S3 will be with respect to that region. Select the region that is closest to the region that your customers belong to so that the data can be fetched faster. The following are the different regions that Amazon provides:

- `GovCloud`
- `US_EAST_1`
- `US_WEST_1`
- `US_WEST_2`
- `EU_WEST_1`
- `EU_CENTRAL_1`
- `AP_SOUTHEAST_1`

- AP_SOUTHEAST_2
- AP_NORTHEAST_1
- SA_EAST_1
- CN_NORTH_1

So, the complete code for initialization is as follows:

```
package com.chapter3;

import com.amazonaws.auth.AWSCredentials;
import com.amazonaws.auth.BasicAWSCredentials;
import com.amazonaws.auth.profile.ProfileCredentialsProvider;
import com.amazonaws.regions.Region;
import com.amazonaws.regions.Regions;
import com.amazonaws.services.s3.AmazonS3;
import com.amazonaws.services.s3.AmazonS3Client;
import com.amazonaws.services.s3.S3ClientOptions;

public abstract class AmazonS3ClientInitializer {
  protected AWSCredentials credentials = null;
  protected AmazonS3 s3 ;

  public AmazonS3ClientInitializer() {
    initializeAWSCredentials();
    initializeAmazonS3Object();
  }

  public void initializeAWSCredentials(){
    System.out.println("================ Initialize AWS
      Credentials ================ ");
    credentials = new BasicAWSCredentials("ACCESS_ID",
      "SECRET_KEY");

    //Path:
    //    LINUX:    /home/sunil/.aws/credentials
    //    WINDOWS:  C:\Users\SUNIL\.aws\credentials
    //credentials = new ProfileCredentialsProvider
      ("sunilgulabani").getCredentials();
  }

  public void initializeAmazonS3Object(){
    System.out.println("================ Initialize Amazon S3
      Object ================ ");
    s3 = new AmazonS3Client(credentials);
```

```
    Region region = Region.getRegion(Regions.AP_SOUTHEAST_1);
    s3.setRegion(region);
    s3.setS3ClientOptions(new
      S3ClientOptions().withPathStyleAccess(true));
  }
}
```

We have made this class abstract so that we can extend this class to different as per functionality. You can alter the design pattern as per your need.

Bucket

Now we will see the implementation part. (For the basics on bucket, please refer to *Chapter 1, Know-How about S3*, and *Chapter 2, S3 using the AWS Management Console*.)

Creating a bucket

`AmazonS3Client` has a method to create a bucket, which is named `s3.createBucket(bucketName);`.

In this method, `bucketName` is the name of your defined bucket.

The complete code for the `CreateBucket` method is as follows:

```
package com.chapter3;

import java.util.Date;

import com.amazonaws.AmazonClientException;
import com.amazonaws.AmazonServiceException;
import com.amazonaws.services.s3.model.Bucket;

public class CreateBucket  extends AmazonS3ClientInitializer{
  public CreateBucket() {
    super();
  }

  public static void main(String[] args) {
    String bucketName = "sg-bucket-2015-using-java-api-" + new
      Date().getTime();

    CreateBucket object = new CreateBucket();
    object.createBucket(bucketName);
    object.listBucket();
```

```
      }

      public void createBucket(String bucketName){
        System.out.println("================= Create Bucket
          ================ ");
        try {
          System.out.println("Bucket Name: " + bucketName + "\n");
          s3.createBucket(bucketName);
        } catch (AmazonServiceException exception) {
          exception.printStackTrace();
        } catch (AmazonClientException exception) {
          exception.printStackTrace();
        }
      }

      public void listBucket(){
        System.out.println("================= Listing Buckets
          ================ ");
        for (Bucket bucket : s3.listBuckets()) {
          System.out.println(" - " + bucket.getName());
        }
      }
    }
```

In the preceding example, after adding the bucket to our Amazon S3 account, we listed all the buckets that are available in our account. Amazon S3 Client uses the s3.listBuckets() method for providing the list of all the buckets.

Creating a bucket with versioning

To enable versioning, the bucket versioning configuration has to be enabled. That configuration request has to be registered at the Amazon S3 Client instance so that the client knows the bucket name for which versioning has to be enabled. This is done as follows:

```
BucketVersioningConfiguration configuration = new
  BucketVersioningConfiguration(BucketVersioningConfiguration.
    ENABLED);

SetBucketVersioningConfigurationRequest request = new
  SetBucketVersioningConfigurationRequest(bucketName, configuration);

s3.setBucketVersioningConfiguration(request);
```

The complete code to create a bucket with the versioning method is as follows:

```java
package com.chapter3;

import java.util.Date;

import com.amazonaws.AmazonClientException;
import com.amazonaws.AmazonServiceException;
import com.amazonaws.services.s3.model.BucketVersioningConfiguration;
import com.amazonaws.services.s3.model.
SetBucketVersioningConfigurationRequest;

public class CreateBucketWithVersioning extends
AmazonS3ClientInitializer {
  public CreateBucketWithVersioning() {
    super();
  }

  public static void main(String[] args) {
    String bucketName = "sg-bucket-2015-" + new Date().getTime() +
      "-with-versioning";

    CreateBucketWithVersioning object = new CreateBucketWith
      Versioning();
    object.createBucketWithVersioning(bucketName);
  }

  public void createBucketWithVersioning(String bucketName){
    System.out.println("================ Create Bucket with
      Versioning =============== ");
    try {
      System.out.println("Bucket Name: " + bucketName + "\n");
      s3.createBucket(bucketName);

      BucketVersioningConfiguration configuration = new
        BucketVersioningConfiguration(BucketVersioning
        Configuration.ENABLED);
      SetBucketVersioningConfigurationRequest request = new
        SetBucketVersioningConfigurationRequest(bucketName,
        configuration);
      s3.setBucketVersioningConfiguration(request);
    } catch (AmazonServiceException exception) {
      exception.printStackTrace();
    } catch (AmazonClientException exception) {
      exception.printStackTrace();
    }
  }
}
```

In the AWS S3 console, we can see that this bucket has been created with versioning enabled:

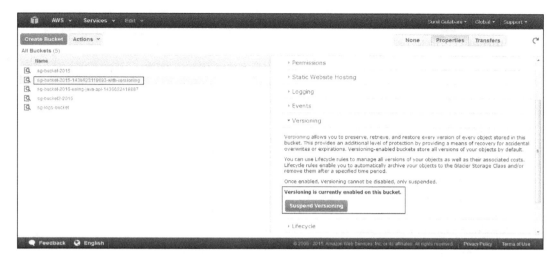

Creating a bucket with logging

To enable the logging mechanism on any bucket, we use `BucketLoggingConfiguration`, and the request has to be registered at Amazon S3 Client:

```
BucketLoggingConfiguration configuration = new
    BucketLoggingConfiguration("sg-logs-bucket", "sg-logs-");

SetBucketLoggingConfigurationRequest request = new
    SetBucketLoggingConfigurationRequest(bucketName, configuration);

s3.setBucketLoggingConfiguration(request);
```

In the preceding code snippet, `"sg-logs-bucket"` is the target bucket name in which the logs will be dumped. The log file prefix will be `"sg-logs-"`, and `bucketName` will be the source bucket name on which the logging mechanism will be enabled.

Along with the target, the bucket should have the `Write` and `ReadAcp` permissions for log delivery. Without having a permission to the target bucket, the logging mechanism won't be enabled. To assign the access control list to the target bucket, we will execute the following code:

```
AccessControlList acl = s3.getBucketAcl("sg-logs-bucket");
```

```
acl.grantPermission(GroupGrantee.LogDelivery,
  Permission.FullControl);

s3.setBucketAcl("sg-logs-bucket", acl);
```

The complete code to create a bucket with logging is as follows:

```
package com.chapter3;

import java.util.Date;

import com.amazonaws.AmazonClientException;
import com.amazonaws.AmazonServiceException;
import com.amazonaws.services.s3.model.AccessControlList;
import com.amazonaws.services.s3.model.BucketLoggingConfiguration;
import com.amazonaws.services.s3.model.GroupGrantee;
import com.amazonaws.services.s3.model.Permission;
import com.amazonaws.services.s3.model.
SetBucketLoggingConfigurationRequest;

public class CreateBucketWithLogging extends
AmazonS3ClientInitializer{
  public CreateBucketWithLogging() {
    super();
  }

  public static void main(String[] args) {
    String bucketName = "sg-bucket-2015-using-java-api-" + new
      Date().getTime() + "-with-logging";

    CreateBucketWithLogging object = new CreateBucketWith
      Logging();
    object.createBucketWithLogging(bucketName);
  }

  public void createBucketWithLogging(String bucketName){
    System.out.println("================ Create Bucket With
      Logging=============== ");
    try {
      System.out.println("Bucket Name: " + bucketName + "\n");
      s3.createBucket(bucketName);


      AccessControlList acl = s3.getBucketAcl("sg-logs-bucket");
      acl.grantPermission(GroupGrantee.LogDelivery,
        Permission.FullControl);
```

```
/*acl.grantPermission(GroupGrantee.LogDelivery,
   Permission.Write);
acl.grantPermission(GroupGrantee.LogDelivery,
   Permission.WriteAcp);
acl.grantPermission(GroupGrantee.LogDelivery,
   Permission.Read);
acl.grantPermission(GroupGrantee.LogDelivery,
   Permission.ReadAcp);*/


s3.setBucketAcl("sg-logs-bucket", acl);

BucketLoggingConfiguration configuration = new
   BucketLoggingConfiguration("sg-logs-bucket", "sg-logs-");
SetBucketLoggingConfigurationRequest request = new
   SetBucketLoggingConfigurationRequest(bucketName,
   configuration);
s3.setBucketLoggingConfiguration(request);

} catch (AmazonServiceException exception) {
exception.printStackTrace();
} catch (AmazonClientException exception) {
exception.printStackTrace();
}
}
}
```

In the AWS S3 console, we can see the bucket has been created with the logging enabled:

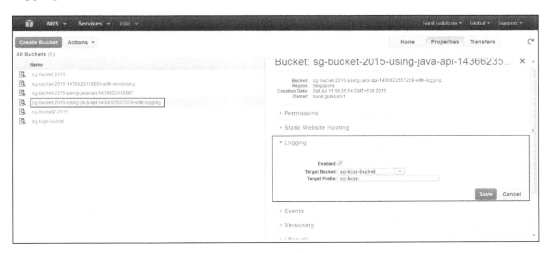

Folder

To create a folder, we need to have a bucket. We cannot create a folder at the root level. Folders can be nested. To create a folder under the bucket, we need to create an object with its content length metadata as 0 and an empty content so that it can be recognized as a folder:

```
ObjectMetadata metadata = new ObjectMetadata();
metadata.setContentLength(0);

InputStream emptyContent = new ByteArrayInputStream(new byte[0]);

PutObjectRequest putObjectRequest = new
  PutObjectRequest(bucketName, folderName + "/", emptyContent,
  metadata);

s3.putObject(putObjectRequest);
```

In the preceding code, you can see that the content length is set to 0, and an empty byte array input has been added. Apart from this, we provided the suffix "/" to the folder name so that we will be able to distinguish between the folder and the object inside the folder.

The following is the complete code to create a folder in a bucket:

```
package com.chapter3;

import java.io.ByteArrayInputStream;
import java.io.InputStream;
import java.util.Date;

import com.amazonaws.AmazonClientException;
import com.amazonaws.AmazonServiceException;
import com.amazonaws.services.s3.model.ListObjectsRequest;
import com.amazonaws.services.s3.model.ObjectListing;
import com.amazonaws.services.s3.model.ObjectMetadata;
import com.amazonaws.services.s3.model.PutObjectRequest;
import com.amazonaws.services.s3.model.S3ObjectSummary;

public class CreateFolderInBucket extends AmazonS3ClientInitializer{
  public CreateFolderInBucket() {
    super();
  }

  public static void main(String[] args) {
    String bucketName = "sg-bucket-2015-using-java-api-" + new
      Date().getTime();
```

```
    String folderName = "sg-folder-" + new Date().getTime();

    CreateFolderInBucket object = new CreateFolderInBucket();
    object.createBucket(bucketName);

    object.createFolderInBucket(bucketName, folderName);

    object.listFolder(bucketName, "sg-folder-");
  }

  public void createFolderInBucket(String bucketName, String
    folderName){
    System.out.println("================ Create Folder In Bucket
      ================ ");
    System.out.println("Folder Name: " + folderName);

    ObjectMetadata metadata = new ObjectMetadata();
    metadata.setContentLength(0);

    InputStream emptyContent = new ByteArrayInputStream(new
      byte[0]);

    PutObjectRequest putObjectRequest = new PutObjectRequest
      (bucketName, folderName + "/", emptyContent, metadata);

    s3.putObject(putObjectRequest);
  }

  public void createBucket(String bucketName){
    System.out.println("================ Create Bucket
      ================ ");
    try {
      System.out.println("Bucket Name: " + bucketName + "\n");
      s3.createBucket(bucketName);
    } catch (AmazonServiceException exception) {
      exception.printStackTrace();
    } catch (AmazonClientException exception) {
      exception.printStackTrace();
    }
  }
}

  public void listFolder(String bucketName, String prefix){
    System.out.println("================ List Bucket with Prefix
      ================ ");
```

```
ListObjectsRequest listObjectsRequest = new ListObjects
  Request()
.withBucketName(bucketName)
.withPrefix(prefix);
ObjectListing objectListing;

do {
  objectListing = s3.listObjects(listObjectsRequest);
  for (S3ObjectSummary objectSummary : objectListing.
    getObjectSummaries()) {
    System.out.println( "\t- " + objectSummary.getKey() + "  "
      + "(size = " + objectSummary.getSize() + ")");
  }
  listObjectsRequest.setMarker(objectListing.getNextMarker());
} while (objectListing.isTruncated());
  }
}
```

Downloading the example code

You can download the example code files for all Packt books you have purchased from your account at http://www.packtpub.com. If you purchased this book elsewhere, you can visit http://www.packtpub.com/support and register to have the files e-mailed directly to you.

In the AWS S3 console, we can see that the bucket and the folder have been created:

Objects

Uploading a file to a bucket

To upload a file to a bucket, we will first create a bucket, and then upload the object into the bucket. Along with uploading the object, we need to assign the **access control list (ACL)** so that a particular user group can access the object. Here we will set the ACL as `PublicRead`:

```
s3.putObject(new PutObjectRequest(
    bucketName,
    fileName,
    new File(filePath))
    .withCannedAcl(CannedAccessControlList.PublicRead));
```

There are other canned access control lists, such as:

* `AuthenticatedRead`
* `BucketOwnerFullControl`
* `BucketOwnerRead`
* `LogDeliveryWrite`
* `Private`
* `PublicRead`
* `PublicReadWrite`

The complete code to upload a file to a bucket is as follows:

```
package com.chapter3;

import java.io.File;
import java.util.Date;

import com.amazonaws.AmazonClientException;
import com.amazonaws.AmazonServiceException;
import com.amazonaws.services.s3.model.CannedAccessControlList;
import com.amazonaws.services.s3.model.ListObjectsRequest;
import com.amazonaws.services.s3.model.ObjectListing;
import com.amazonaws.services.s3.model.PutObjectRequest;
import com.amazonaws.services.s3.model.S3ObjectSummary;

public class UploadFileInBucket extends AmazonS3ClientInitializer{
    public UploadFileInBucket() {
```

```
        super();
    }

    public static void main(String[] args) {
        String bucketName = "sg-bucket-2015-using-java-api-" + new
            Date().getTime();

        UploadFileInBucket object = new UploadFileInBucket();
        object.createBucket(bucketName);

        object.uploadFileInBucket(bucketName, "C:\\admin.ico",
            "admin.ico");
        object.listAllFolderAndObjectsInBucket(bucketName);
    }

    public void uploadFileInBucket(String bucketName, String
        filePath, String fileName){
        System.out.println("================= Upload File In Bucket
            ================ ");
        // upload file to folder and set it to public
        System.out.println("fileName: " + fileName);
        s3.putObject(new PutObjectRequest(
            bucketName,
            fileName,
            new File(filePath))
            .withCannedAcl(CannedAccessControlList.PublicRead));
    }

    public void createBucket(String bucketName){
        System.out.println("================= Create Bucket
            ================ ");
        try {
            System.out.println("Bucket Name: " + bucketName + "\n");
            s3.createBucket(bucketName);
        } catch (AmazonServiceException exception) {
            exception.printStackTrace();
        } catch (AmazonClientException exception) {
            exception.printStackTrace();
        }
    }

    public void listAllFolderAndObjectsInBucket(String bucketName){
        System.out.println("================= List Bucket's Folders And
            Objects ================ ");
        ListObjectsRequest listObjectsRequest = new
            ListObjectsRequest()
            .withBucketName(bucketName);
```

```
ObjectListing objectListing;

do {
  objectListing = s3.listObjects(listObjectsRequest);
  for (S3ObjectSummary objectSummary :
    objectListing.getObjectSummaries()) {
    System.out.println( "\t- " + objectSummary.getKey() + "   "
      + "(size = " + objectSummary.getSize() + ")");
  }
  listObjectsRequest.setMarker(objectListing.getNextMarker());
} while (objectListing.isTruncated());
  }
}
```

In the preceding code, we listed the folder and objects under the bucket using the `ListObjectsRequest` method.

In the AWS S3 console, we can see that the object (`admin.ico`) has been added to the bucket:

Uploading a file to a folder

To upload a file to a folder, we will create a bucket, create a folder inside the bucket, and then upload the file to the folder with the help of the following code:

```
String fileName = folderName + "/" + fileNameSuffix;

s3.putObject(new PutObjectRequest(
  bucketName,
```

```
        fileName,
        new File(filePath))
    .withCannedAcl(CannedAccessControlList.PublicRead));
```

The only difference here is that the file name has the name of the folder as a prefix.

The complete code to upload a file to a folder is as follows:

```
package com.chapter3;

import java.io.File;
import java.util.Date;

import com.amazonaws.AmazonClientException;
import com.amazonaws.AmazonServiceException;
import com.amazonaws.services.s3.model.CannedAccessControlList;
import com.amazonaws.services.s3.model.ListObjectsRequest;
import com.amazonaws.services.s3.model.ObjectListing;
import com.amazonaws.services.s3.model.PutObjectRequest;
import com.amazonaws.services.s3.model.S3ObjectSummary;

public class UploadFileInBucket extends AmazonS3ClientInitializer{
    public UploadFileInBucket() {
        super();
    }

    public static void main(String[] args) {
        String bucketName = "sg-bucket-2015-using-java-api-" + new
            Date().getTime();

        UploadFileInBucket object = new UploadFileInBucket();
        object.createBucket(bucketName);

        object.uploadFileInBucket(bucketName,"C:\\admin.ico",
            "admin.ico");
        object.listAllFolderAndObjectsInBucket(bucketName);
    }

    public void uploadFileInBucket(String bucketName, String
        filePath, String fileName){
        System.out.println("================= Upload File In Bucket
            ================ ");
        // upload file to folder and set it to public
        System.out.println("fileName: " + fileName);
        s3.putObject(new PutObjectRequest(
            bucketName,
```

```
      fileName,
      new File(filePath))
      .withCannedAcl(CannedAccessControlList.PublicRead));
  }

  public void createBucket(String bucketName){
    System.out.println("================ Create Bucket
      ================ ");
    try {
      System.out.println("Bucket Name: " + bucketName + "\n");
      s3.createBucket(bucketName);
    } catch (AmazonServiceException exception) {
      exception.printStackTrace();
    } catch (AmazonClientException exception) {
      exception.printStackTrace();
    }
  }

  public void listAllFolderAndObjectsInBucket(String bucketName){
    System.out.println("================ List Bucket's Folders And
      Objects ================ ");
    ListObjectsRequest listObjectsRequest = new ListObjects
      Request()
    .withBucketName(bucketName);
    ObjectListing objectListing;

    do {
      objectListing = s3.listObjects(listObjectsRequest);
      for (S3ObjectSummary objectSummary : objectListing.
        getObjectSummaries()) {
          System.out.println( "\t- " + objectSummary.getKey() + "
            " + "(size = " + objectSummary.getSize() + ")");
      }
      listObjectsRequest.setMarker(objectListing.
        getNextMarker());
    } while (objectListing.isTruncated());
  }
}
```

In the AWS S3 console, we can see that the object (`admin.ico`) has been added to the folder:

Listing of bucket, folder, and objects

We first fetch the entire S3 bucket list, then we iterate over the objects of the bucket, and if it contains the folder, then we iterate over the objects of the folder.

The complete code for listing is as follows:

```
package com.chapter3;

import com.amazonaws.services.s3.model.Bucket;
import com.amazonaws.services.s3.model.ListObjectsRequest;
import com.amazonaws.services.s3.model.ObjectListing;
import com.amazonaws.services.s3.model.S3ObjectSummary;

public class ListFullHierarchy extends AmazonS3ClientInitializer{
  public ListFullHierarchy() {
    super();
  }

  public static void main(String[] args) {
    new CreateBucket().createBucket("sg-bucket-2015");
    new CreateBucketWithLogging().createBucketWithLogging("sg-
      bucket-2015-with-logging");
    new CreateBucketWithVersioning().createBucketWithVersioning
      ("sg-bucket-2015-with-versioning");
```

```
    new CreateFolderInBucket().createFolderInBucket("sg-bucket-
        2015", "sg-folder");
    new UploadFileInBucket().uploadFileInBucket("sg-bucket-
        2015","C:\\admin.ico","admin.ico");
    new UploadFileInFolder().uploadFileInFolder("sg-bucket-2015",
        "sg-folder","C:\\admin.ico","admin.ico");

    ListFullHierarchy object = new ListFullHierarchy();
    object.listFullHierarchy();
}

public void listFullHierarchy(){
    System.out.println("================= Listing Full Hierarchy
        ================= ");
    for (Bucket bucket : s3.listBuckets()) {
        System.out.println(" - " + bucket.getName());
        ListObjectsRequest listObjectsRequest = new
            ListObjectsRequest().withBucketName(bucket.getName());
        ObjectListing objectListing;
        do {
            objectListing = s3.listObjects(listObjectsRequest);
            for (S3ObjectSummary objectSummary :
                objectListing.getObjectSummaries()) {
                System.out.println( "\t\t- " + objectSummary.getKey() +
                    "  " + "(size = " + objectSummary.getSize() + ")");
            }
            listObjectsRequest.setMarker(objectListing.
                getNextMarker());
        } while (objectListing.isTruncated());
    }
}
```

In the preceding code, we created the bucket and the folder, and then uploaded objects to the folder and the bucket. Then we listed the full hierarchy of the bucket, folder, and objects that have been added in our Amazon S3 account.

Delete operations

For deleting a bucket, the primary condition is that the bucket should be empty. So we will now see how to delete the object, the folder, and then the bucket. To delete an object/folder, execute the following command:

```
s3.deleteObject(bucketName, OBJECT_KEY_OR_FOLDER_NAME);
```

Or execute the following command:

```
s3.deleteObject(new DeleteObjectRequest(bucketName,
    OBJECT_KEY_OR_FOLDER_NAME));
```

Replace bucketName with the actual bucket name and OBJECT_KEY_OR_FOLDER_NAME with either your object key or the name of the folder that is supposed to be deleted.

The complete code for delete operations on buckets, folders, and objects is as follows:

```
package com.chapter3;

import java.util.List;

import com.amazonaws.services.s3.model.DeleteObjectRequest;
import com.amazonaws.services.s3.model.ListObjectsRequest;
import com.amazonaws.services.s3.model.ObjectListing;
import com.amazonaws.services.s3.model.S3ObjectSummary;

public class DeleteOperations extends AmazonS3ClientInitializer{

    public DeleteOperations() {
        super();
    }

    public static void main(String[] args) {
        DeleteOperations object = new DeleteOperations();

        object.deleteFolderAndItsObjects("sg-bucket-2015", "sg-
            folder");
        object.deleteObjectInBucket("sg-bucket-2015","admin.ico");
        object.deleteBucketObjects("sg-bucket-2015");
        object.deleteBucket("sg-bucket-2015");
    }

    public void deleteObjectInBucket(String bucketName, String
        fileKey){
        System.out.println("================= Delete Object In Bucket
            ================= ");
        System.out.println(" - bucket: " + bucketName);
        System.out.println("\t- fileKey: " + fileKey);

        s3.deleteObject(new DeleteObjectRequest(bucketName, fileKey));
    }

    public void deleteBucket(String bucketName){
```

```
      System.out.println("================ Delete Bucket
        =============== ");
      System.out.println(" - bucket: " + bucketName);

      s3.deleteBucket(bucketName);
    }

    public void deleteBucketObjects(String bucketName){
      System.out.println("================ Delete Bucket Object
        =============== ");
      ListObjectsRequest listObjectsRequest = new
        ListObjectsRequest().withBucketName(bucketName);
      ObjectListing objectListing;
      System.out.println(" - " + bucketName);
      do {
        objectListing = s3.listObjects(listObjectsRequest);
        for (S3ObjectSummary objectSummary :
          objectListing.getObjectSummaries()) {
          System.out.println("\t- " + objectSummary.getKey());
          s3.deleteObject(bucketName, objectSummary.getKey());
        }
        listObjectsRequest.setMarker(objectListing.getNextMarker());
      } while (objectListing.isTruncated());
    }

    public void deleteFolderAndItsObjects(String bucketName, String
      folderName) {
      System.out.println("================ Delete Bucket Folder and
        it's Object =============== ");
      System.out.println(" - " + bucketName);
      System.out.println("\t- " + folderName);
      List<S3ObjectSummary> fileList = s3.listObjects(bucketName,
        folderName).getObjectSummaries();
      for (S3ObjectSummary objectSummary : fileList) {
        System.out.println("\t\t- " + objectSummary.getKey());
        s3.deleteObject(bucketName, objectSummary.getKey());
      }
      s3.deleteObject(bucketName, folderName);
    }
  }
```

Here we have demonstrated the code that can be used to delete a single bucket, a folder, or the content of the folder and bucket.

Summary

In this chapter, you learned how to use Amazon SDK Java for Amazon S3 web services. The API is meant to make things easy for developers so that they can concentrate on the actual business logic, and integrate the Amazon S3 API easily. You learned how to create, upload, get, and delete a bucket, folder, and objects.

In the next chapter, you will learn how to copy objects from one bucket to another, manage the lifecycle of the bucket, and use cross-origin resource sharing with the Amazon S3 Java SDK.

4
S3 using AWS SDK – Java (Part 2)

In the previous chapter, you learned the basic operations for buckets, folders, and objects using the Amazon SDK Java. Now we will discuss some more operations other than add, update, delete, and get. In this chapter, we will cover the following topics:

- Copying objects from one bucket to another using different methods
- Managing the lifecycle of a bucket
- Cross-origin resource sharing

Let's see how to can manage Amazon S3 using Amazon SDK—Java.

Copying objects

Amazon S3 SDK provides a copy object functionality that allows you to copy Amazon S3 objects from one bucket to another. For this, you have to define the source bucket name, source object key, destination bucket name, and the destination object key. The following is the API that we can use to copy the object:

```java
public void copyObjects1(String sourceBucketName, String
   sourceObjectKey, String destinationBucketName, String
   destinationObjectKey) {
   System.out.println("================ COPY OBJECT
      ================ ");
   try {
     s3.copyObject(sourceBucketName, sourceObjectKey,
        destinationBucketName, destinationObjectKey);
   } catch (AmazonServiceException exception) {
     exception.printStackTrace();
```

```
    } catch (AmazonClientException exception) {
      exception.printStackTrace();
    }
  }
```

We can also copy objects using the `CopyObjectRequest` class. This is used when we want to add the metadata of a newly copied object along with `CannedAccessControlList` and constraints.

```
public void copyObjects2(String sourceBucketName, String
  sourceObjectKey, String destinationBucketName, String
  destinationObjectKey){
    System.out.println("================ COPY OBJECT USING
      CopyObjectRequest =============== ");
    try {
      CopyObjectRequest copyObject = new
        CopyObjectRequest(sourceBucketName, sourceObjectKey,
        destinationBucketName, destinationObjectKey);
      s3.copyObject(copyObject);
    } catch (AmazonServiceException exception) {
      exception.printStackTrace();
    } catch (AmazonClientException exception) {
      exception.printStackTrace();
    }
  }
```

The following is the complete source code for `Copy` object:

```
// import statements

public class CopyObjects extends AmazonS3ClientInitializer{

  public CopyObjects() {
    super();
  }

  public static void main(String[] args) {
    CopyObjects main = new CopyObjects();

    String sourceBucketName = "sg-copy-object" ;
    String sourceObjectKey = "AmazonS3ClientInitializer.java";
    main.createBucket(sourceBucketName);
    main.uploadFileInBucket(sourceBucketName, "/home/sunil
      /workspace/Chapter4S3/src/com/chapter4/AmazonS3
      ClientInitializer.java", sourceObjectKey);
```

```java
        String destinationBucketName = sourceBucketName + "-copy-1";
        main.createBucket(destinationBucketName);
        String destinationObjectKey = "AmazonS3ClientInitializer-copy-
            1.java";

        main.copyObjects1(sourceBucketName, sourceObjectKey,
            destinationBucketName, destinationObjectKey);

        destinationObjectKey = "AmazonS3ClientInitializer-copy-
            2.java";
        main.copyObjects2(sourceBucketName, sourceObjectKey,
            destinationBucketName, destinationObjectKey);

        main.listAllFolderAndObjectsInBucket(destinationBucketName);
    }

    public void copyObjects1(String sourceBucketName, String
        sourceObjectKey, String destinationBucketName, String
        destinationObjectKey){

        // Same as shown in the last code snippet
    }

    public void copyObjects2(String sourceBucketName, String
        sourceObjectKey, String destinationBucketName, String
        destinationObjectKey){

        // Same as shown in the last code snippet
    }

    public void uploadFileInBucket(String bucketName, String
        filePath, String fileName){

        // Same as shown in the previous chapter
    }

    public void createBucket(String bucketName){
        // Same as shown in the previous chapter
    }

    public void listAllFolderAndObjectsInBucket(String bucketName){
        // Same as shown in the previous chapter
    }
}
```

```
/**
  Output:

  ================ Initialize AWS Credentials ================
  ================ Initialize Amazon S3 Object ================
  ================ Create Bucket ================
  Bucket Name: sg-copy-object

  ================ Upload File In Bucket ================
  fileName: AmazonS3ClientInitializer.java
  ================ Create Bucket ================
  Bucket Name: sg-copy-object-copy-1

  ================ COPY OBJECT ================
  ================ COPY OBJECT USINg CopyObjectRequest
     ================
  ================ List Bucket's Folders And Objects
     ================
  - AmazonS3ClientInitializer-copy-1.java  (size = 1402)
  - AmazonS3ClientInitializer-copy-2.java  (size = 1402)
*/
```

As we can see in the AWS Management S3 console, the source and destination buckets have been created, and an object that we uploaded in the source bucket was copied into the destination bucket.

In this example, sg-copy-object is the source bucket, and sg-copy-object-copy-1 is the destination bucket:

In the source folder `sg-copy-object`, we uploaded the `AmazonS3ClientInitializer.java` object:

Both the files, `AmazonS3ClientInitializer-copy-1.java` and `AmazonS3ClientInitializer-copy-2.java`, are copied into the `sg-copy-object-copy-1` bucket.

Amazon SDK also provides an API for a multipart upload that can be used when the file size is big. The following things are used for a multipart upload:

- `InitiateMultipartUploadRequest`: This is used to specify the destination bucket name and the object key for a multipart upload.

- `InitiateMultipartUploadResult`: This provides the result of `InitiateMultipartUploadRequest`, which contains the upload ID.

- `partSizeInBytes`: This specifies the part size that we will transfer. For our demo, we have specified 1 MB as the part size. You can increase this as per the need.

- `bytePositionInBytes`: This is used to specify the first byte that is to be copied in `CopyPartRequest`.

- `objectSizeInBytes`: This is the total size of the source object.

- `CopyPartRequest`: This is used to copy part of the source object to the destination object in a multipart upload.

- `CopyPartResult`: This contains the result of `CopyPartRequest`. It maintains the responses that have `ETags`.

- `ETag`: This is the entity tag that is a hash of the object's content. This hash is not the MD5 digest.

- `CompleteMultipartUploadResult`: This contains the response of the file multipart upload.

Let's see the full source code for copying an object using a multipart upload:

```
package com.chapter4;

// import statements
public class MultipartCopyObjects extends AmazonS3Client
  Initializer{

  public MultipartCopyObjects() {
    super();
  }

  public static void main(String[] args) {
    MultipartCopyObjects main = new MultipartCopyObjects();

    String sourceBucketName = "sg-m1-copy-object" ;
    main.createBucket(sourceBucketName);

    String sourceObjectKey = "AmazonS3ClientInitializer.java";
    main.uploadFileInBucket(sourceBucketName,
    "/home/sunil/workspace/Chapter4S3/src/com/chapter4/
    AmazonS3ClientInitializer.java", sourceObjectKey);

    String destinationBucketName = sourceBucketName + "-copy-1";
    main.createBucket(destinationBucketName);
```

```
    String destinationObjectKey = "AmazonS3ClientInitializer-copy-
      1.java";

    main.copyObjects3(sourceBucketName, sourceObjectKey,
      destinationBucketName, destinationObjectKey);

    main.listAllFolderAndObjectsInBucket(destinationBucketName);
  }

public void copyObjects3(String sourceBucketName, String
  sourceObjectKey,String destinationBucketName, String
  destinationObjectKey){
  System.out.println("================ COPY OBJECT USING
    MULTIPART ================ ");
  List<CopyPartResult> copyPartResultList = new
    ArrayList<CopyPartResult>();

  /**
  * InitiateMultipartUploadRequest is used to specify the
    destination bucket name and the object key for multipart
    upload.
  */
  InitiateMultipartUploadRequest initiateMultipartUploadRequest
    = new InitiateMultipartUploadRequest(destinationBucketName,
    destinationObjectKey);

  /**
  * InitiateMultipartUploadResult provides the result of
    InitiateMultipartUploadRequest which contains the upload ID.
  */
  InitiateMultipartUploadResult initMultipartUploadResult =
    s3.initiateMultipartUpload(initiateMultipartUploadRequest);
  try {
    /**
    * the part size that we will transfer. For our demo we gave
      1 MB. You can increase as per the need.
    */
    long partSizeInBytes = getBytesFromMB(1);

    /**
    * This will specify the first byte to be copied in
      CopyPartRequest.
    */
    long bytePositionInBytes = 0;
```

```java
    /**
     * This is the total size of the source object.
     */
    long objectSizeInBytes = getSourceObjectLength
      (sourceBucketName, sourceObjectKey);

    CopyPartRequest copyPartRequest = null;

    CopyPartResult copyPartResult = null;

    for (int i = 1; bytePositionInBytes < objectSizeInBytes;
      i++){
      copyPartRequest = getCopyPartRequest(
        sourceBucketName, sourceObjectKey,
        destinationBucketName, destinationObjectKey,
        initMultipartUploadResult.getUploadId(),
        bytePositionInBytes, partSizeInBytes, objectSizeInBytes,
          i);

      copyPartResult = s3.copyPart(copyPartRequest);
      copyPartResultList.add(copyPartResult);
      bytePositionInBytes += partSizeInBytes;
    }

    List<PartETag> partEtags = getPartEtags(copyPartResultList);

    CompleteMultipartUploadResult completeMultipartUploadResult
      =
    s3.completeMultipartUpload(new CompleteMultipartUpload
      Request(
      destinationBucketName, destinationObjectKey,
      initMultipartUploadResult.getUploadId(), partEtags));

    System.out.println("Bucket Name: " +
      completeMultipartUploadResult.getBucketName());
    System.out.println("Key: " + completeMultipartUpload
      Result.getKey());
  } catch (Exception e) {
    System.out.println(e.getMessage());
  }
}

private long getBytesFromMB(int mb){
  return mb*1024*1024;
}
```

```
private long getSourceObjectLength(String sourceBucketName,
    String sourceObjectKey){
    return s3.getObjectMetadata(new GetObjectMetadataRequest
        (sourceBucketName, sourceObjectKey)).getContentLength();
}

/**
*   CopyPartRequest is used to copy part of the source object to
    a destination object in multipart upload.
*/
private CopyPartRequest getCopyPartRequest(
    String sourceBucketName, String sourceObjectKey,
    String destinationBucketName, String destinationObjectKey,
    String uploadId, long bytePositionInBytes,
    long partSizeInBytes, long objectSizeInBytes, int partNumber
){
    CopyPartRequest copyPartRequest = new CopyPartRequest();

    copyPartRequest.withSourceBucketName(sourceBucketName);
    copyPartRequest.withSourceKey(sourceObjectKey);

    copyPartRequest.withDestinationBucketName
        (destinationBucketName);
    copyPartRequest.withDestinationKey(destinationObjectKey);

    copyPartRequest.withUploadId(uploadId);
    copyPartRequest.withFirstByte(bytePositionInBytes);

    if(bytePositionInBytes + partSizeInBytes -1 >=
        objectSizeInBytes){
        copyPartRequest.withLastByte(objectSizeInBytes - 1);
    }else{
        copyPartRequest.withLastByte(bytePositionInBytes +
            partSizeInBytes - 1);
    }

    copyPartRequest.withPartNumber(partNumber);
    return copyPartRequest;
}

/**
* ETag is the entity tag which is hash of the object's content.
* This hash is not the MD5 digest.
* @param responses
* @return
```

```
*/
private List<PartETag> getPartEtags(List<CopyPartResult>
   responses){
   List<PartETag> partEtags = new ArrayList<PartETag>();
   for (CopyPartResult response : responses){
     partEtags.add(new PartETag(response.getPartNumber(),
        response.getETag()));
   }
   return partEtags;
}

public void uploadFileInBucket(String bucketName, String
   filePath, String fileName){
   System.out.println("================ Upload File In Bucket
     ================ ");
   // upload file to folder and set it to public
   System.out.println("fileName: " + fileName);
   s3.putObject(new PutObjectRequest(
     bucketName,
     fileName,
     new File(filePath))
     .withCannedAcl(CannedAccessControlList.PublicRead));
}

public void createBucket(String bucketName){
   // Same as shown in the previous chapter

}

public void listAllFolderAndObjectsInBucket(String bucketName){
   // Same as shown in the previous chapter

}
}
/**
Output:

================ Initialize AWS Credentials ================
================ Initialize Amazon S3 Object ================
================ Create Bucket ================
Bucket Name: sg-m-copy-object

================ Upload File In Bucket ================
fileName: AmazonS3ClientInitializer.java
```

```
================ Create Bucket ================
Bucket Name: sg-m-copy-object-copy-1


================ COPY OBJECT USING MULTIPART ================
Bucket Name: sg-m-copy-object-copy-1
Key: AmazonS3ClientInitializer-copy-1.java
================ List Bucket's Folders And Objects
    ================
- AmazonS3ClientInitializer-copy-1.java  (size = 1402)


*/
```

As you can see in the AWS Management S3 console, the source and destination buckets have been created, and an object that we uploaded in the source bucket is copied into the destination bucket.

In this example, `sg-m-copy-object` and `sg-m-copy-object-copy-1` are the two buckets that we've created:

In `sg-m-copy-object`, we uploaded the object `AmazonS3ClientInitializer.java`:

Using the multipart API, we copied `sg-m-copy-object/`
`AmazonS3ClientInitializer.java` to `sg-m-copy-object-copy-1` as
`AmazonS3ClientInitializer-copy-1.java`:

Bucket lifecycle

Amazon S3 SDK also provides an API for managing the lifecycle of a bucket. It has
two ways to manage the objects of the bucket:

- Transition
- Removal

The transition method moves the data to Amazon Glacier, whereas the removal method removes the data from Amazon S3.

To add the lifecycle, we need to apply rules to the bucket. We can apply multiple rules to a single bucket. Let's see how we create rules:

```
private Rule createRule(String id, String prefix, int days){
  Rule rule = new Rule();
  rule.withId(id);
  rule.withPrefix(prefix);

  /**
   * Transition is to archive objects into Amazon Glacier.
   */
  rule.withTransition(new Transition()
  .withDays(days)
  .withStorageClass(StorageClass.Glacier));

  rule.withStatus(BucketLifecycleConfiguration.ENABLED.
    toString());

  return rule;
}
```

There are some rules that need to be applied to the bucket lifecycle configuration. Multiple rules can be applied to a bucket. Rules can be formed with several parameters depending on the requirements. We can also provide expirationDate or expirationInDays to form a rule:

```
rule.withExpirationDate(expirationDate);
rule.withExpirationInDays(expirationInDays);
```

To apply a rule to the bucket, we have the following API:

```
public void addBucketLifeCycleConfiguration(String bucketName){
  Rule archiveRule = createRule("Archive in 0 days",
    "archived/",0);

  List<Rule> rulesList = new ArrayList<Rule>();
  rulesList.add(archiveRule);

  BucketLifecycleConfiguration configuration = new
    BucketLifecycleConfiguration();
  configuration.withRules(rulesList);

  s3.setBucketLifecycleConfiguration(bucketName, configuration);
}
```

The full source code for a bucket lifecycle is as follows:

```java
package com.chapter4;

// import statements

public class LifeCycleOfObject extends AmazonS3ClientInitializer{
  public LifeCycleOfObject(){
    super();
    s3.setRegion(Region.getRegion(Regions.US_EAST_1));
  }

  public static void main(String[] args) {
    LifeCycleOfObject main = new LifeCycleOfObject();
    String bucketName = "sg-lifecycle";
    main.createBucket(bucketName);
    main.addBucketLifeCycleConfiguration(bucketName);
    main.getBucketLifecycleConfiguration(bucketName);
    /*main.deleteBucketLifecycleConfiguration(bucketName);
    main.getBucketLifecycleConfiguration(bucketName);*/

    //    main.deleteBucket(bucketName);
  }

  public void addBucketLifeCycleConfiguration(String bucketName){
    // as shown in the last code snippet

  }

  public void getBucketLifecycleConfiguration(String bucketName){
    System.out.println("================= GET BUCKET LIFECYCLE
      CONFIGURATION =============== ");
    BucketLifecycleConfiguration configuration = s3.getBucket
      LifecycleConfiguration(bucketName);
    if(configuration!=null){
      List<Rule> rulesList = configuration.getRules();
      for(Rule rule : rulesList){
        System.out.println("Id: " + rule.getId());
        System.out.println("Prefix: " + rule.getPrefix());
        System.out.println("Status: " + rule.getStatus());
      }
    }else{
      System.out.println("No Bucket Life Cycle Configuration
        Found.");
    }
```

```
    }

    public void deleteBucketLifecycleConfiguration(String
      bucketName){
      System.out.println("================ DELETE BUCKET LIFECYCLE
        CONFIGURATION =============== ");
      s3.deleteBucketLifecycleConfiguration(bucketName);
    }

    private Rule createRule(String id, String prefix, int days){
      // As shown in the last code snippet

    }

    public void createBucket(String bucketName){
      // Same as shown in the previous chapter

    }

    public void deleteBucket(String bucketName){
     // Same as shown in the previous chapter

    }
}

/**
  Output

  ================ Initialize AWS Credentials ================
  ================ Initialize Amazon S3 Object ================
  =============== Create Bucket ================
  Bucket Name: sg-lifecycle

  ================ ADD BUCKET LIFECYCLE CONFIGURATION
    ================
  ================ GET BUCKET LIFECYCLE CONFIGURATION
    ================
  Id: Archive in 0 days
  Prefix: archived/
  Status: Enabled

*/
```

As seen in the following screenshot, the rule that we mentioned in the preceding code has been applied in the properties of the `sg-lifecycle` bucket, under the lifecycle menu. You can manage the rule from both ends — using code as well as the management console.

Cross-origin Resource Sharing

Cross-origin Resource Sharing (**CORS**) is used for sharing resources between different domains. We can use the resources of one domain in another domain by keeping the CORS support enabled. CORS is achieved by creating rules and assigning those rules to the bucket.

First of all, we need to create `CORSRule`:

```
. . . .
CORSRule.AllowedMethods[] allowedMethods1 = new CORSRule.
AllowedMethods[] {CORSRule.AllowedMethods.GET, CORSRule.
AllowedMethods.PUT,
CORSRule.AllowedMethods.POST, CORSRule.AllowedMethods.DELETE};

String[] allowedOrigins1 = new String[]
  {"http://*.sunilgulabani.com"};

CORSRule rule1 = createRule("Sunil Gulabani Website
  Rule",allowedOrigins1,allowedMethods1,null,-1);

. . . .
private CORSRule createRule(
  String id,
```

```
        String[] allowedOrigins,
        CORSRule.AllowedMethods[] allowedMethods,
        String[] exposedHeaders,
        int maxAgeSeconds
    ){
        System.out.println("================ CREATE RULE
          =============== ");
        CORSRule rule = new CORSRule();

        rule.withId(id);

        if(allowedOrigins!=null && allowedOrigins.length > 0)
        rule.withAllowedOrigins(Arrays.asList(allowedOrigins));

        if(allowedMethods!=null && allowedMethods.length > 0)
        rule.withAllowedMethods(Arrays.asList(allowedMethods));

        if(maxAgeSeconds!= -1){
            rule.withMaxAgeSeconds(maxAgeSeconds);
        }

        if(exposedHeaders!=null && exposedHeaders.length > 0){
            rule.withExposedHeaders(Arrays.asList(exposedHeaders));
        }

        return rule;
    }
    ....
```

In the preceding code, we've created a rule allowing the methods: GET, PUT, POST, and DELETE.

The origin that can access it is http://*.sunilgulabani.com. You can define multiple origin names as per your requirements.

exposedHeaders identifies a header in the response. Max Age Seconds specifies the time in seconds that your browser can cache.

Let's see the full source code:

```
    package com.chapter4;

    // import statements

    public class CrossOriginResourceSharing extends AmazonS3Client
        Initializer{
```

```java
public CrossOriginResourceSharing(){
  super();
}

public static void main(String[] args) {
  CrossOriginResourceSharing main = new CrossOrigin
    ResourceSharing();
  String bucketName = "sg-cors";
  main.createBucket(bucketName);
  main.addCORS(bucketName);
  main.listCORSConfig(bucketName);
  //    main.deleteCORS(bucketName);
  //    main.listCORSConfig(bucketName);
  //    main.deleteBucket(bucketName);
}

private CORSRule createRule(
  String id,
  String[] allowedOrigins,
  CORSRule.AllowedMethods[] allowedMethods,
  String[] exposedHeaders,
  int maxAgeSeconds
){
  // Same as shown in last code snippet

}

public void addCORS(String bucketName){
  System.out.println("================ ADD CORS ================
    ");
  BucketCrossOriginConfiguration configuration = new
    BucketCrossOriginConfiguration();

  List<CORSRule> rules = new ArrayList<CORSRule>();

  CORSRule.AllowedMethods[] allowedMethods1 = new
    CORSRule.AllowedMethods[] {CORSRule.AllowedMethods.GET,
    CORSRule.AllowedMethods.PUT, CORSRule.AllowedMethods.POST,
    CORSRule.AllowedMethods.DELETE};
  String[] allowedOrigins1 = new String[]
    {"http://*.sunilgulabani.com"};
  CORSRule rule1 = createRule("Sunil Gulabani Website
    Rule",allowedOrigins1,allowedMethods1,null,-1);

  CORSRule.AllowedMethods[] allowedMethods2 = new
    CORSRule.AllowedMethods[] {CORSRule.AllowedMethods.GET,
    CORSRule.AllowedMethods.POST};
```

```
    String[] allowedOrigins2 = new String[] {"*"};
    CORSRule rule2 = createRule("Third Party Website
      Rule",allowedOrigins2,allowedMethods2,null,1000);

    rules.add(rule1);
    rules.add(rule2);
    configuration.setRules(rules);

    s3.setBucketCrossOriginConfiguration(bucketName,
      configuration);
}

public void deleteCORS(String bucketName){
  System.out.println("================ DELETE CORS
    =============== ");
  s3.deleteBucketCrossOriginConfiguration(bucketName);
}

public void listCORSConfig(String bucketName){
  System.out.println("================ LIST CORS
    =============== ");
  BucketCrossOriginConfiguration configuration =
    s3.getBucketCrossOriginConfiguration(bucketName);

  if (configuration == null){
    System.out.println("Configuration is null.");
    return;
  }else{
    for (CORSRule rule : configuration.getRules()){
      System.out.println("Id: " + rule.getId());

      if(rule.getAllowedOrigins()!=null){
        System.out.println("Allowed Origins: ");
        for(String allowedOrigin : rule.getAllowedOrigins()){
          System.out.println("\t-" + allowedOrigin);
        }
      }

      if(rule.getAllowedMethods()!=null){
        List<AllowedMethods> allowedMethodsList =
          rule.getAllowedMethods();
        System.out.println("Allowed Methods: ");
        for(AllowedMethods allowedMethods : allowedMethodsList){
          System.out.println("\t-" + allowedMethods.toString());
        }
      }
```

```java
      if(rule.getAllowedHeaders()!=null){
        System.out.println("Allowed Headers: ");
        for(String allowedHeaders: rule.getAllowedHeaders()){
          System.out.println("\t-" + allowedHeaders);
        }
      }

      if(rule.getExposedHeaders()!=null){
        System.out.println("Expose Header: ");
        for(String exposedHeaders : rule.getExposedHeaders()){
          System.out.println("\t-" + exposedHeaders);
        }
      }

      System.out.println("Max Age Seconds: " +
        rule.getMaxAgeSeconds());

      System.out.println("-------------------------------------
      ----------");
    }
  }
}

public void createBucket(String bucketName){

  // Same as shown in the previous chapter

}

public void deleteBucket(String bucketName){
  // Same as shown in the previous chapter

}
}
/**
  Output

  =============== Initialize AWS Credentials ===============
  =============== Initialize Amazon S3 Object ===============
  =============== Create Bucket ===============
  Bucket Name: sg-cors

  =============== ADD CORS ===============
  =============== CREATE RULE ===============
  =============== CREATE RULE ===============
  =============== LIST CORS ===============
  Id: Sunil Gulabani Website Rule
```

```
Allowed Origins:
-http://*.sunilgulabani.com
Allowed Methods:
  -GET
  -PUT
  -POST
 -DELETE
Max Age Seconds: 0
------------------------------------------------
Id: Third Party Website Rule
Allowed Origins:
  -*
Allowed Methods:
  -GET
  -POST
Max Age Seconds: 1000
------------------------------------------------
=============== DELETE CORS ===============
=============== LIST CORS ===============
Configuration is null.
=============== Delete Bucket ===============
 - bucket: sg-cors

*/
```

We can manage the CORS rules from the AWS S3 Management Console as well:

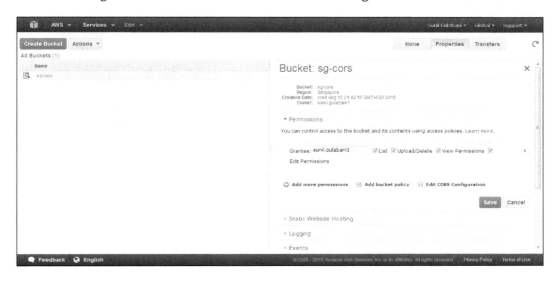

In the preceding screenshot, we can see the `bucket sg-cors` that we created.

Now, click on **Bucket** and then on **Properties**. Then under `Permissions`, click **on Edit CORS Configuration**:

We can see the CORS configuration consists of the same configuration that we created programmatically. Thus, you can use either of the two ways to change the CORS configurations.

Summary

In this chapter, you learned how to copy objects. You also learned to use the multipart file upload feature for copying large-sized objects. We discussed the bucket lifecycle, which can be defined in two ways — transition (move to Glacier) and removal. Last but not least, you learned about the CORS configuration, which is used to provide access via different domains. By now you are well-informed about Amazon S3, and you know how to manage amazon S3 using Amazon S3 SDK — Java. In the next chapter, you will learn how to host your static website over Amazon S3.

5
Deploying a Website on S3

Until now, we have seen how to manage buckets, folders, and objects and process operations on them. In this chapter, we will discuss how to deploy our static website on Amazon S3 and access it. We will consider the configuration using the AWS Management Console and the Amazon S3 Java SDK.

Website configuration using the Amazon S3 Java SDK

In previous chapters, we saw how to create a bucket and upload objects (files) to the bucket. Here, we will take a look at how we can create a new bucket, upload `index.html` and `error.html` files, and configure the website for the bucket.

To set the bucket website configuration, we have a method in Amazon S3, as follows:

```
s3.setBucketWebsiteConfiguration(bucketName,new
    BucketWebsiteConfiguration(indexHTML, errorHTML));
```

Here, `bucketName` the name of our bucket, in which the website source code will be added. The `indexHTML` and `errorHTML` parameters are the landing and error pages, respectively, which are specified to the bucket website configuration. In case an error occurs, the `errorHTML` page will be displayed.

To get the bucket website configuration, we have a method in AmazonS3, which is as follows:

```
BucketWebsiteConfiguration configuration =
    s3.getBucketWebsiteConfiguration(bucketName);
```

Here, `bucketName` will be passed, and we need to fetch its bucket website configuration.

To delete the bucket website configuration, we have a method in Amazon S3, which is as follows:

```
s3.deleteBucketWebsiteConfiguration(bucketName);
```

Here, bucketName will be passed, and we need to delete its bucket website configuration.

Here's the full source code:

```
// all import statements
public class SetupWebsite extends AmazonS3ClientInitializer{
  public SetupWebsite() {
    super();
  }

  public static void main(String[] args) {
    SetupWebsite mainApp = new SetupWebsite();
    String bucketName = "sg-website";
    mainApp.createBucket(bucketName);

    String indexHTML = "index.html" ;
    String errorHTML = "error.html" ;
    mainApp.uploadFileInBucket(bucketName, "index.html",
      indexHTML);
    mainApp.uploadFileInBucket(bucketName, "error.html",
      errorHTML);

    mainApp.getConfiguration(bucketName);
    mainApp.setConfiguration(bucketName, indexHTML, errorHTML);
    mainApp.getConfiguration(bucketName);
//    mainApp.deleteConfiguration(bucketName);
//    mainApp.deleteBucket(bucketName);
  }

  public BucketWebsiteConfiguration getConfiguration(String
    bucketName){
    ....................
  }

  public void setConfiguration(String bucketName, String
    indexHTML, String errorHTML){
    ....................
  }
```

```
    public void deleteConfiguration(String bucketName){
        .....................
    }

    public void createBucket(String bucketName){
        .....................
    }

    public void deleteBucket(String bucketName){
        .....................
    }

    public void uploadFileInBucket(String bucketName, String
        filePath, String fileName){
        .....................
    }
}
/**
OUTPUT:

================ Initialize AWS Credentials ================
================ Initialize Amazon S3 Object ================
================ Create Bucket ================
Bucket Name: sg-website

================ Upload File In Bucket ================
fileName: index.html
================ Upload File In Bucket ================
fileName: error.html
================ Get Bucket Website Configuration ================
No configuration found for this bucket: sg-website
================ Set Bucket Website Configuration ================
Bucket Name: sg-website
Index HTMLindex.html
Error HTMLerror.html
================ Get Bucket Website Configuration ================
Index Document Suffix: index.html
Error Document: error.html

*/
```

In the AWS Management Console, we will see that the bucket has been created, and the two files that we added—`input.html` and `error.html`—exist, as in the following screenshot:

For the bucket website configuration, we can take a look at the properties of the bucket under the **Static Website Hosting** tab. In the following screenshot, **Enable website hosting** is selected and the values are set:

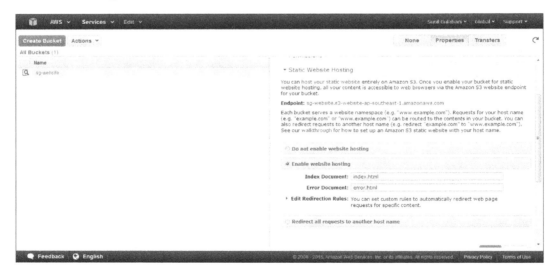

Also, we need to provide the bucket policy, which can be added from the **Permissions** tab. The bucket policy will look similar to the following code:

```
{
    "Version": "2012-10-17",
    "Statement": [
        {
            "Sid": "AddPerm",
            "Effect": "Allow",
            "Principal": "*",
            "Action": "s3:GetObject",
            "Resource": "arn:aws:s3:::sg-website.com/*"
        }
    ]
}
```

To access this, we can get the URL from the **Static Website Hosting** tab itself, specified as **Endpoint**. In our case, we have one of the following:

- `sg-website.s3-website-ap-southeast-1.amazonaws.com`
- `sg-website.s3-website-ap-southeast-1.amazonaws.com/index.html`

When we access the URL in a browser, it will show the content of `index.html` as in the following screenshot:

If we provided any other suffix in the URL, it would open the error page.

For instance, when we try to access the following URL, the error page is displayed because a file with this name doesn't exist in the bucket:

`http://sg-website.s3-website-ap-southeast-1.amazonaws.com/index.htmlasdasd`

In this way, we can add as many pages as we want and provide links to access these over the Internet. You can even upload files from the AWS Management Console and change the respective landing and error pages from the bucket's properties under the **Static Website Hosting** tab.

Mapping a custom domain with website configuration in Amazon S3

First of all, we need a domain name to display our static website that is hosted on Amazon S3. The domain name can be used for any of the domain providers. For our example, we purchased the domain from Route 53 (`tweakings3.com`). You can take a look at the hosted zone under Route 53 in the AWS Management Console. As we bought the domain from Route 53, it created an entry for the hosted zone as well. Otherwise, we would have needed to manually create the hosted zone and enter the namespace of the DNS provider.

For the static website content, we need to create two buckets: one bucket is for `www.tweakings3.com` and another for `tweakings3.com`. This would be helpful if a user tries to open the website by either URL.

We added the `index.html` and `error.html` pages to both our website buckets. After adding the HTML, don't forget to make it public; this is required for other users to access it. Then, add the bucket policy to access the bucket content as follows:

```
{
    "Version": "2012-10-17",
    "Statement": [
      {
        "Sid": "AddPerm",
        "Effect": "Allow",
        "Principal": "*",
        "Action": "s3:GetObject",
        "Resource": "arn:aws:s3:::tweakings3.com/*"
      }
    ]
}
```

Now, we will configure the **Static Website Hosting** property for both the buckets. Here, we will select the **Enable website hosting** option and add the respective filename, `index.html` or `error.html`, and save it:

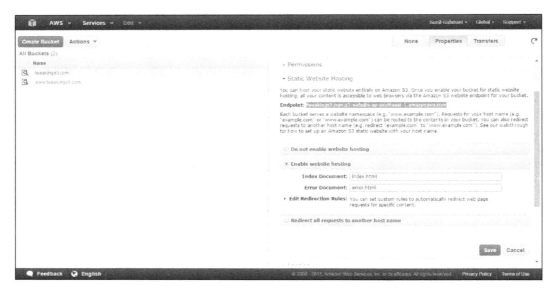

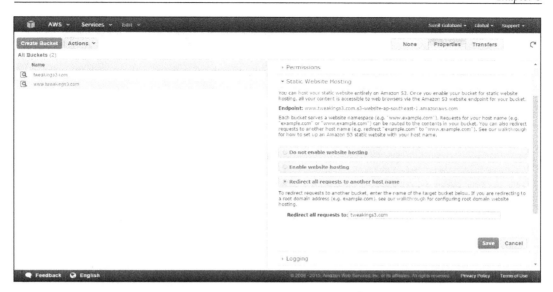

Try running the URL specified in the **Static Website Hosting** tab. The content of `index.html` should be displayed as follows:

So, using the URLs, we can get the content of index.html. Now, we will configure Route 53 to map the domain name with the S3 endpoint bucket, tweakings3.com. To do this, go to the Route 53 dashboard. Here, click on **Create Record Set** to add the **A – Ipv4 address** record set for tweakings3.com and www.tweakings3.com:

Mask the **Alias Hosted Zone ID** value with black (similar to the previous image):

After adding the A record set, it will get registered, and accessing the URL, either
`tweakings3.com` or `www.tweakings3.com`, should open the page:

Summary

In this chapter, you learned to configure the static website hosting along with the bucket
itself. Then, we discussed how to map our custom domain name with the bucket.
Overall, in this book, we considered operations for all buckets, folders, and objects, and
in this last chapter, we operated on hosting a website with a custom domain name.

Index

G

Graphical User Interface (GUI) 9

I

index.html file
  URL 24
index.html object
  URL 25
initialization
  about 37
  BasicAWSCredentials used 37
  ProfileCredentialsProvider used 37-40

K

keys 4

M

multipart upload
  about 63, 64
  used, for copying objects 64-70

O

object operations
  about 20, 21
  Reduced Redundancy Storage, using 21
  Server Side Encryption, using 22-25
objects
  about 3, 4
  copying, from one bucket to another 59-63
  copying, multipart upload used 64-70
  deleting 55-57
  listing 54, 55

P

ProfileCredentialsProvider
  using 37-40

R

Reduced Redundancy Storage (RRS)
  about 5
  using 21
Representational State Transfer (REST)
  web service 5
Route 53 86

S

Server Side Encryption
  using 22-25
Simple Object Access Protocol (SOAP)
  web service 5

V

versioning 26, 27

W

website, configuring
  Amazon S3 Java SDK used 81-86
  in Amazon S3, custom domain
    mapping with 86-91

Thank you for buying
Amazon S3 Essentials

About Packt Publishing

Packt, pronounced 'packed', published its first book, *Mastering phpMyAdmin for Effective MySQL Management*, in April 2004, and subsequently continued to specialize in publishing highly focused books on specific technologies and solutions.

Our books and publications share the experiences of your fellow IT professionals in adapting and customizing today's systems, applications, and frameworks. Our solution-based books give you the knowledge and power to customize the software and technologies you're using to get the job done. Packt books are more specific and less general than the IT books you have seen in the past. Our unique business model allows us to bring you more focused information, giving you more of what you need to know, and less of what you don't.

Packt is a modern yet unique publishing company that focuses on producing quality, cutting-edge books for communities of developers, administrators, and newbies alike. For more information, please visit our website at www.packtpub.com.

About Packt Open Source

In 2010, Packt launched two new brands, Packt Open Source and Packt Enterprise, in order to continue its focus on specialization. This book is part of the Packt Open Source brand, home to books published on software built around open source licenses, and offering information to anybody from advanced developers to budding web designers. The Open Source brand also runs Packt's Open Source Royalty Scheme, by which Packt gives a royalty to each open source project about whose software a book is sold.

Writing for Packt

We welcome all inquiries from people who are interested in authoring. Book proposals should be sent to author@packtpub.com. If your book idea is still at an early stage and you would like to discuss it first before writing a formal book proposal, then please contact us; one of our commissioning editors will get in touch with you.

We're not just looking for published authors; if you have strong technical skills but no writing experience, our experienced editors can help you develop a writing career, or simply get some additional reward for your expertise.

Amazon S3 Cookbook

ISBN: 978-1-78528-070-2   Paperback: 280 pages

Over 30 hands-on recipes that will get you up and running with Amazon Simple Storage Service (S3) efficiently

1. Learn how to store, manage, and access your data with AWS SDKs.

2. Study the Amazon S3 pricing model and learn how to calculate costs by simulating practical scenarios.

3. Optimize your Amazon S3 bucket by following step-by-step instructions of how to deliver your content with CloudFront, secure the S3 bucket with IAM, and lower costs with object life cycle management.

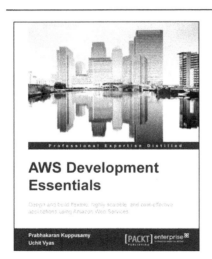

AWS Development Essentials

ISBN: 978-1-78217-361-8   Paperback: 226 pages

Design and build flexible, highly scalable, and cost-effective applications using Amazon Web Services

1. Integrate and use AWS services in an application.

2. Reduce the development time and billing cost using the AWS billing and management console.

3. This is a fast-paced tutorial that will cover application deployment using various tools along with best practices for working with AWS services.

Please check **www.PacktPub.com** for information on our titles

OpenStack Essentials

ISBN: 978-1-78398-708-5   Paperback: 182 pages

Demystify the cloud by building your own private OpenStack cloud

1.   Set up a powerful cloud platform using OpenStack.

2.   Learn about the components of OpenStack and how they interact with each other.

3.   Follow a step-by-step process that exposes the inner details of an OpenStack cluster.

Implementing Cloud Storage with OpenStack Swift

ISBN: 978-1-78216-805-8   Paperback: 140 pages

Design, implement, and successfully manage your own cloud storage cluster using the popular OpenStack Swift software

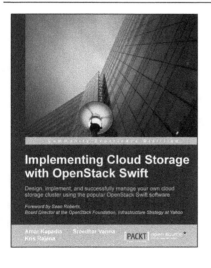

1.   Learn about the fundamentals of cloud storage using OpenStack Swift.

2.   Explore how to install and manage OpenStack Swift along with various hardware and tuning options.

3.   Perform data transfer and management using REST APIs.

Please check **www.PacktPub.com** for information on our titles

www.ingramcontent.com/pod-product-compliance
Lightning Source LLC
Chambersburg PA
CBHW060159060326
40690CB00018B/4167